Philosophies of Research into Higher Education

Also available from Continuum

Philosophy of Educational Research, Richard Pring

Researching Education, David Scott and Robin Usher

End of Knowledge in Higher Education, Ronald Barnett

Research in Higher Education

Rethinking Universities, Sally Baker and Brian J. Brown

Dispositional Theory of Good Teaching, John Fazey

Teaching in Higher Education, John Fazey and Eben Muse

Philosophies of Research into Higher Education

Brian J. Brown and Sally Baker

continuum

Continuum International Publishing Group
The Tower Building
11 York Road
London SE1 7NX

80 Maiden Lane
Suite 704
New York
NY 10038

www.continuumbooks.com

British Library Cataloguing-in-Publication Data
A catalogue record for this book is available from the British Library.

ISBN: 978-0-8264-9417-7 (hardcover)

Library of Congress Cataloging-in-Publication Data
A catalog record for this book is available from the Library of Congress.

Typeset by Servis Filmsetting Ltd, Manchester
Printed and bound in Great Britain by
Biddles Ltd, King's Lynn, Norfolk

'For Xylia. Also for John and Della –
for all that you have done'

Contents

1

Theories of knowledge and theories of society

This book represents both an academic and a personal journey. It is concerned, as its title suggests, with research in education, with particular reference to the higher education sphere. It is born out of our frustration with the relationship between research, practice and policy in the field of higher education. We began our journey from the premise that surely it would be a good idea if the way we taught – indeed if the way that education establishments went about their business – could be done better, more efficiently and with a greater likelihood of happiness for practitioners and learners. From this position we began looking for ways in which research, practice and policy could be made to converge.

This path soon led to frustration. This was despite the recent burgeoning of research into higher education, including the UK's growing research industry concerned with how participation in higher education can be enhanced and research related to the mechanics of teaching students with special needs – research which could enhance the growing number of courses intended to prepare budding academics for the teaching experience in universities, colleges and elsewhere. Researchers are clearly engaged in the process of trying to do something useful.

So why is it taking so long for an evidence-based spirit to take hold in education? In other public services, including healthcare, criminal justice and social care, the enthusiasts for evidence-based practice have made far greater inroads into the ethos of their disciplines. So why is it difficult in education?

When we conceived of this volume, we entertained hopes that research into higher education could be more useful, innovative and better designed if we were clearer about the philosophical and epistemological basis of the theories that underlie our research methods. People who have to interpret and apply research would do a better job if they were able to interrogate research more critically and appreciate its strengths and weaknesses. This volume would therefore attempt to provide this information for an audience of researchers, policy-makers, students and lecturers in higher education.

However, this first flush of optimism has been tempered by experience. Partly, this is because we as yet do not fully understand the relationship between research and educational practice. Researchers and educators do not simply need to learn more about each other – though it would be nice if they did – but there are fundamental problems of understanding that relate to the rather different traditions of thinking that inform research and practice. Moreover, in education especially, there is considerable variation in the meaning of even the most basic terms. The discussion of what human enquiry involves is given interesting twists by the sheer variety of senses and moral connotations that the community has attached to terms like 'positivism', 'realism', 'empiricism' and so on. These have often drifted so far from their original moorings that it is hard to predict what they will mean when anyone uses them.

Our purpose then is partly to clarify what all this represents, but also we will try to show the relevance of understanding the philosophical basis for research activity and we will, more ambitiously, try to explain how the assumptions people make inform the kinds of questions they ask and the techniques used to answer them. Researchers, practitioners and policy-makers often have tacit theories about what works, what happens and what matters in the social world, and while these seldom find their way explicitly into formal research reports, they can make a big difference to the way things turn out.

The potential for research to inform policy and practice in higher education is growing as never before, yet the pathway from research findings to effective change is often far from easy. Evidence is being called for to solve problems as diverse as the recruitment of students, stress in staff, and learning in the classroom. Yet there is often little sense of how such research should be done or how its findings could be made to matter. Policy-makers can sometimes barely conceal their frustration at not finding research which can hit the nail on the head of the questions that they want answering. How can all that public money have been spent with so little to show for it? The problem is not that research has *not* been done, or that it is 'poor quality' in any simple sense, but that researchers and policy-makers are often starting from different sets of assumptions.

Drawing on our interest in the history and philosophy of knowledge, we will argue that to make sense of research and to use it wisely, practitioners need to understand the thinking behind traditions of enquiry and beliefs about research methods. The contrasting strands of different investigative traditions will be critically described; and the reader will be familiarized with the contribution of positivism, hypothesis testing, realism, interpretativism and postmodernism and the contribution they can make to interpreting research, and to planning and conducting one's own. By understanding research in this way, the most advantageous use can be made of the diverse theories, thinking tools and practical techniques that research involves and the results can benefit teachers, learners and policy-makers in the higher education arena. There is, said Kurt Lewin sagely, 'nothing so practical as a good theory'.

Therefore, a good deal of this book will involve providing outlines and critical discussions of the key concepts and philosophical approaches to research in the higher education systems of developed nations. As post-compulsory education expands to include an ever-higher proportion of the population, and institutions are eagerly exploiting new markets for degree-level education, it is vital that we explore new ways of understanding this process. The imperatives which are driving policy-makers and educators towards evidence-based or evidence-informed practice mean that taking stock of what our research methods are based on is an increasingly vital task. Now that evidence-based approaches are gaining popularity in higher education practice and policy it is appropriate to reflect on what they mean, and more importantly what the data they yield might mean for practice in administering degree programmes, recruiting students and providing an education for an increasingly large segment of the population.

This book offers the reader an approach to understanding higher education and research within it in a way that attends to underlying theoretical perspectives, and which enables readers to critically appreciate the role of research in higher education policy and practice. With the development of mass higher education in the UK we urgently need to intellectualize the debates about teaching, learning and widening participation, and to understand how inquiries into the philosophies of science can be useful in illuminating higher education systems. So far, philosophers of science and knowledge have tended to confine their inquiries to physics, cosmology or social theory, and there has been little work so far that allows us to understand enquiry in higher education in this way. This groundbreaking book will allow readers to understand the relevance of social theory, epistemology, the philosophy of science and gain a critical understanding of research methods and approaches to making sense of higher education. It will be essential reading for those interested in how we can research the increasingly complex array of factors that determine the success of the higher education enterprise and the well-being of students within it.

This chapter will outline some of the key theories of the role of knowledge in society and its relationship to other social and political structures. Many figures in contemporary social theory have contributions to make to our understanding of what a university means and what research on the higher education process should involve. For example, Weber, Parsons, Habermas, Gadamer, Lyotard, Foucault and Bourdieu have all made contributions to our understanding of knowledge, culture information and discourse, yet their contributions are often forgotten in the dash to achieve results or implement policy. This chapter, therefore, outlines these contributions and identifies their role in generating a more sophisticated approach to research in this field.

We shall see more of these figures later. For the moment, let us note that these theorists who have had something to say about the education system are crucial in framing the terms of any debate on the role of education. A pervasive theme in the work of social theorists is that education does something – it accomplishes something for that society. This idea was particularly apparent in the work of Talcott Parsons in the middle of the twentieth century. In a series of publications (e.g. Parsons 1937, 1951) he expounded his thoughts on the function of educational institutions in society. His chief concern was to try to understand how social order or social equilibrium was maintained. Education had a major part to play in this process. In the early years it manages the transition on the part of children from the highly particularistic world of the family to the more universalistic world of society as a whole where students would, in his view, achieve their status based on merit or worth. In the later years of education, institutions such as schools and colleges adapted people into occupational roles through a process of socialization.

Parsons attached great importance to the functions of phenomena such as education and other social processes and social institutions in American society. Parsons borrowed the idea of function from anthropology 'as a way of talking about the consequences of any given pattern or patterns of social interaction for the stability and ongoingness of systems of interaction (Johnson 1993: 117). Parsons tended to view these patterns and functions as contributing to the relatively smooth functioning of society, which he saw as a hierarchy of interlocking and mutually constitutive systems. At a time when American society was driven by recession, racial segregation (including in the education system), and later by Senator McCarthy's anti-communism, Parsons was mesmerized by a vision of order and consensus. The shared values and norms and the generally agreed-upon means for accomplishing collectively desirable ends were viewed by Parsons as being functional for the operation of society as a system. The education system itself operates as a mechanism that 'functions to allocate these human resources within the role-structure of adult society'. Thus educational establishments, by training, testing and evaluating students, match their dispositions, capacities, talents and skills to the available jobs for which they are best suited. Education is therefore seen as the major mechanism for role allocation.

While few would now claim to be Parsonians, it is easy to see the residues of his approach at work in contemporary policy. Efforts to align the skills of school or university leavers with the presumed needs of the knowledge economy presuppose a systemic fit between the world of education and the world of work.

Hans-Georg Gadamer, by contrast, is associated with a very different focus of interest in education. Rather than focusing upon its larger scale functions in making up the social whole, he continually returns to the metaphor of conversation to think about how we may come to understand the topic at hand. As Gadamer puts it, conversation:

> is a process of two people understanding each other. Thus it is a characteristic of every true conversation that each opens himself to the other person, truly accepts his point of view as worthy of consideration and gets inside the other to such an extent that he understands not a particular individual, but what he says. The thing that has to be grasped is the objective rightness or otherwise of his opinion, so that they can agree with each other on a subject.
>
> (Gadamer 1979: 347)

The key feature here is how knowledge is conceptualized. In Gadamer's view of conversation, knowledge is not a fixed entity or commodity to be grasped. It is not something 'out there' awaiting discovery in any simple sense. Instead, knowledge is seen as an aspect of a process. Knowledge arises out of interaction. Gadamer uses the metaphor of a horizon: the participants in the conversation bring prejudices or pre-judgments to the encounter, which he calls their own 'horizon of understanding'. This is 'the range of vision that includes everything that can be see from a particular vantage point' (Gadamer 1979: 143). These pre-judgments and understandings enable our involvement in what is being said. In the ideal type of conversation he advocates, we try to understand a horizon that is not our own in relation to our own. These kinds of conversations involve putting our own understandings and pre-judgments to the test. 'Only by seeking to learn from the "other", only by fully grasping its claims upon one can it be critically encountered' (Bernstein 1991: 4). This involves sustaining an openness to the full power of what the 'other' has to say. 'Such an opening does not entail agreement but rather the to-and-fro play of dialogue' (Bernstein 1991: 4). Through this process of dialogue at its best we can seek to discover other peoples' standpoints and horizons. In so doing, we might find that their ideas become intelligible, without our necessarily having to agree with them (Gadamer 1979: 270). In other words, we can come to terms with the other (Crowell 1990: 358). In this conversational model, the concern is not to 'win the argument', but instead to promote understanding and human well-being. In this view, agreement cannot be imposed, but is achieved through common understanding (Habermas 1984: 285–7). In doing this, the understanding we bring from the past is challenged against encounters with the present and forms a new synthesis that we take into the future (Louden 1991: 106). This synthesis is sometimes referred to as a 'fusion of horizons'.

> The horizon of the present is being continually formed, in that we have continually to test all our prejudices. An important part of that testing is the encounter with the past and the understanding of the tradition from which we come . . . In a tradition this process of fusion is continually going on, for there old and new continually grow together to make something of living value, without either being explicitly distinguished from the other.
>
> (Gadamer 1979: 273)

Some have suggested that this notion of fusion overstates the degree of harmony and consensus in many educational or conversational encounters. Thus 'fusion' may not be quite the right word. It does not entirely fit the 'ruptures that disturb our attempts to reconcile different ethical–political horizons' (Bernstein 1991: 10). However, what these theorists are trying to describe, perhaps, is the sense of satisfaction, enjoyment or achievement after a really good conversation where we feel we have learned something. In a sense, this theorizing is an attempt to ring-fence that process and say that there is something special about it which we desperately need in education.

Both the accounts of educational processes we have seen above, in their contrasting ways, provide idealized accounts of what education is and what it can do. In contrast to this focus on social systems with neatly interlocking functions and the satisfactions of open dialogue, let us turn to the curiously prescient and somewhat dystopian visions of Jean-Francois Lyotard (1984), whose book *The Postmodern Condition: A report on knowledge* was written a generation ago. Despite this, and the fact that it was published a decade before Tim Berners-Lee was credited with the invention of the internet, Lyotard's dystopian vision looks strangely like the contemporary university system.

Lyotard begins from the premise or working hypothesis 'that the status of knowledge is altered as societies enter what is known as the post-industrial age and cultures enter what is known as the postmodern age' (Lyotard 1984: 3). This trend towards deindustrialization in the West has been in progress since the end of the 1950s, but for Lyotard, what is interesting are the consequences for knowledge. Knowledge has become a major force of production in itself in the two decades since Lyotard's book was published, and his prediction was that knowledge would increasingly be translated into quantities of information, with corresponding changes in the process of research itself. Already in 1984, Lyotard was able to see that 'the miniaturization and commercialization of machines is already changing the way in which learning is acquired, classified, made available, and exploited' (1984: 4). In highly computerized societies knowledge is becoming 'exteriorized' from knowers. In previous times, it was assumed that knowledge and pedagogy were inextricably linked, but in the contemporary world this has been replaced by a notion of knowledge as a *commodity*:

> Knowledge is and will be produced in order to be sold, it is and will be consumed in order to be valorized in a new production: in both cases, the goal is exchange. Knowledge ceases to be an end in itself, it loses its 'use-value'. (Lyotard 1984: 4–5)

Lyotard continues:

> Knowledge in the form of an informational commodity indispensable to productive power is already, and will continue to be, a major – perhaps *the* major – stake in the worldwide competition for power. It is conceivable that the nation-states will one day fight for control of information, just as they battled in the past for control over territory, and afterwards for control of access to and exploitation of raw materials and cheap labour. (1984: 5)

As large organizations and capital become more multinational, the idea of an autonomous, sovereign nation-state begins to look old-fashioned and rather difficult to sustain. New technologies will hasten and reinforce these developments as they facilitate the transfer of commercially valuable knowledge between producers and customers. The machinery of government of the old nation-states, predicts Lyotard, will come to be perceived as an impediment, as 'a factor of opacity and "noise"' (1984: 5) and as an obstacle to the full commercialization of knowledge. The old fashioned idea that 'learning falls within the purview of the State, as the mind or brain of society' will give way to the view that 'society exists and progresses only if the messages circulating within it are rich in information and easy to decode' (1984: 5). Consequently, Lyotard predicted an important shift in the system of organized learning:

> It is not hard to visualize learning circulating along the same lines as money, instead of for its 'educational' value or political (administrative, diplomatic, military) importance; the pertinent distinction would no longer be between knowledge and ignorance, but rather, as is the case with money, between 'payment knowledge' and 'investment knowledge' – in other words, between units of knowledge exchanged in a daily maintenance framework (the reconstitution of the work force, 'survival') versus funds of knowledge dedicated to optimizing the performance of a project. (1984: 6)

Lyotard (1984: 9), like Foucault, is convinced that knowledge and power are 'two sides of the same question'. People's reliance on narrative knowledge in the past will come to be seen as increasingly archaic, and in powerful quarters in the West will come to be supplanted by scientific knowledge. The latter is 'governed by the demand for legitimation' and, in line with the imperialist spirit of Western civilization, will not accept anything that 'fails to conform to the rules (the requirement for proof or argumentation) of its own language game' (1984: 27). Scientific knowledge, then, is progressively more commodified, and its adequacy is judged against a universal epistemological 'gold standard'. Narratives, by contrast, are legitimated in much more local, specific and particular terms by the simple fact that they 'do what they do' (1984: 23).

In the age of information technology, 'the question of knowledge is now more than ever a question of government' (1984: 9). Lyotard anticipates that the function of the state will change so that machines will come to play an important role in regulatory and reproductive processes. The power to make decisions will tend to be determined by the question of who has access to information (1984: 14). In this dystopia, eventually researchers and academics will no longer be needed since most of the work they presently do will be undertaken by computerized data network systems (1984: 53).

This vision of a knowledge dystopia, where commercialized knowledge flows and automated knowledge production predominate, with a concomitant deskilling of researchers and academics as their roles are taken over by automated processes, is a valuable picture to bear in mind when confronted with optimistic talk about 'knowledge economies'.

Finally, in our tour through the selected theories of what knowledge and education involve, let us pause for a moment with Pierre Bourdieu. His work has a particular significance for educational researchers and has given us concepts that are immensely valuable. Bourdieu originally gained popularity among British educationalists in the 1970s when he took his place at the head of a new tribe of 'sociologists of education'. While his publications cover a whole range of other topics and fields including economics, art and aesthetics, philosophy, politics, and history and geography, education is a theme to which he constantly returned throughout a long working life. Volumes such as *Homo Academicus*

(1988), *La Noblesse d'Etat* (*The State Nobility*) (1996), his riposte to scholastic reason in *Pascalian Meditations* (2000) and *La Misère du Monde* (1993), translated as *The Weight of the World* (1999), contain a number of accounts from both teachers and students on what it was like to be involved in education in France.

In much of his work, Bourdieu invites us to attend to symbolic structures, and to consider their relation to both the cognitive and emotional structures of the individual and social structures of society. Particularly relevant to our purposes, he draws our attention to language, categorizations and labels, and their systems of production and mode of consumption. These he feels are critical in the reproduction and transformation of the social world. Three major assumptions run through Bourdieu's work (Bourdieu and Wacquant 1992: 12–14). First, he believes that individuals' mental schemata are a kind of embodiment of social divisions, distinctions and categorizations. In other words, the social and the cognitive are inextricably linked. Thus, an analysis of social phenomena and structures logically carries through into an analysis of objective dispositions. Second, this correspondence between social and mental structures serves important political functions. It means that symbolic systems can be instruments of domination, not simply instruments of knowledge. The categories with which the social world is perceived, imposing themselves 'with all appearances of objective necessity' (Bourdieu and Wacquant 1992: 13), decisively reinforce the social order. Accepting the idea that symbolic systems are social products that constitute social relations, Bourdieu suggests that one can transform the world by transforming its representation, to some extent. Following on from this is Bourdieu's third main assumption: systems of classification are sites of struggle between individuals and groups. Social taxonomies such as ethnic groups, occupations, class groups, cultural identities and so on are the result of and at stake in social power relations. In this view, it becomes important therefore to consider how language and, more broadly, 'symbolic goods' contribute to the reproduction and transformation of structures of domination.

There are two further concepts of Bourdieu's which deserve elaboration in this context and which may well allow us to make sense of what is happening, for example, in healthcare. The first is that of the 'field', a set of social relations within which the social drama is played out, and the second is the 'habitus', which describes the mode of conduct of the social actors.

Field

Fields, according to Bourdieu, are 'networks of social relations, structured systems of social positions within which struggles or manoeuvers take place over resources, stakes and access' (Bourdieu 1990). Scheuer (2003: 145) adds a definition of a 'field', as 'a structured network of social practices and positions related to a trade or area of production'. Therefore, different healthcare practitioners can be perceived as occupying different fields depending upon how much capital they have acquired through the amount of clinical governance language and social practice that they are able to perform. Chouliaraki and Fairclough (1999) argue that Bourdieu's decision to differentiate between fields enables 'empirical investigation of shifts in the social practices of late modernity' to be conducted (1999: 101), which is aligned with the aim of examining the shifting communicative patterns of healthcare to be examined. Fields can be thought of as a kind of market or game (*jeu*) because, in a field, we have stakes (*enjeux*), an investment (*illusio*), and we also have trump cards (Bourdieu and Wacquant 1992: 98). Fields are occupied by two sets of actors, the dominant and the dominated, who attempt to usurp, exclude and establish monopoly over the mechanisms of the field's reproduction and the type of power effective in it (Bourdieu and Wacquant 1992: 106). Fields are dynamic social microcosms, forever changing, and require a study approach that recognizes their relational or dialectical qualities (1992: 96). The field, then, comprises the social totality of the relevant actors (DiMaggio and Powell 1983: 149), not on simply what occurs 'within the healthcare encounter' or 'within the profession'. Furthermore, when one comes to think in terms of field, one comes to focus on power, domination and class. One might suggest, as does Drummond (1998), that healthcare organizations are best seen as subfields, or as embedded in a larger field, and are enclosed in a social universe with its own laws of functioning. This enables us to see the healthcare setting, like a field, as a space in which a game takes place, or as a field of relations between individuals who are competing for personal or own-group advantage.

Habitus

The players in the field are not simply infinitely re-transforming themselves according to where their advantage lies. They play according to a personal disposition or '*habitus*'. This is their characteristic style of play which enables them to be recognized by what they say, do, wear or how they carry themselves. *Habitus* is the 'durably inculcated system of structured, structuring dispositions' found within a field (Bourdieu 1990: 52). *Habitus* is embodied within individual social actors. It is 'the social inscribed in the body . . . a feel for or sense of the "social game" . . . the source of most practices . . . a tendency to generate regulated behaviours apart from any reference to rules' (Bourdieu 1962: 111). *Habitus* exists in the form of mental and corporeal schemata, a matrix of perception, appreciation and action (Bourdieu and Wacquant 1992: 16–18). In short, *habitus* pervades or saturates social processes (Foster 1986: 105). One might have the *habitus* of a teacher, a student, an entrepreneur and so on. A *habitus* might pertain to a class group, a sporting subculture or an occupational culture. Some researchers are also talking about institutional *habitus*. Reay *et al.* (2001) argue that, in relation to higher education choices, a 'school effect' or 'institutional habitus' interacts with the students' class, gender and ethnic background to affect secondary school pupils' and further education college students' lives in relation to the education system. Institutional *habitus*, says Thomas (2002), is more than merely the overt culture of the educational institution – it refers to relational issues and priorities which are deeply embedded and not necessarily something of which the actors are conscious. There is a complex game involved in succeeding, summarized by Robbins (1993: 153):

> Bourdieu's conclusion seemed to suggest that the working-class students were at an unfair disadvantage and that there was a conspiratorial collusion between middle-class staff and middle-class students which meant that these students received a structurally preferential treatment which was a kind of cheating.

Like a field, *habitus* is not static as it is a combination of the social actor's more deeply ingrained identity, with his or her more transient identities as a health professional, patient, student, parent and so on (Meisenhelder 1997). The *habitus* is also always changing because it is constantly exposed to new experiences, many of which are reinforcing, but often modify it over a period of time (Bourdieu and Wacquant 1992: 133). *Habitus* also changes because of changes in the climate of the field, and changes in the kinds of capital available and the struggles over them. Even apparently trivial aspects of academic life can make sense in this framework. The question of feedback on student coursework is interesting because it offers the potential for a transfer of habits from a dominant group to a subordinate one in the academy. In a study by Weaver (2006), students identified unhelpful feedback as that which was too general and lacking in detail, as highlighted by the following remarks:

> . . . two-word notes at the side of the report didn't help much.
>
> . . . we usually had a tick or something circled to say something was wrong.
>
> Usually we could work out what went wrong but some analysis of what was lacking would have helped in future assessments.
>
> . . . although there was feedback, it was not particularly detailed.
>
> (Weaver 2006: 387)

This corresponded to tutors' comments, such as: '. . . you have got the important stuff right', 'there are certain sections which could have been better supported . . .', and 'a sound answer generally' (Weaver 2006: 387). Thus, while feedback is provided, it can, through being cryptic, contain the implicit message that 'my time is more valuable than yours – you'll have to work it out' and, while going through the motions of being helpful, it can end up restricting the craft knowledge of academic life to those in the know.

Although society may be 'in the individual as the *habitus*' (Meisenhelder 1997: 180), *habitus* is also constitutive of the field, working in a dialectic fashion, as an infinite yet strictly limited generative capacity, as determinism and freedom, conditioning and creativity, and consciousness and the unconscious (Bourdieu 1990: 55). As Bourdieu notes: 'the field, as a structured space, tends to structure the *habitus*, while the *habitus* tends to structure the perceptions of the field' (Bourdieu 1988: 784). *Habitus* may appear in differing ways: as a 'collective *habitus* – a unifying cultural code; a 'dispositional *habitus*' – an internalized cultural code; or as a 'manifest *habitus*' the practice of a characteristic style (Nash 1990: 434).

The *habitus* may not be at all obvious to the people who embody and display it: 'meanings and consequences of action are not transparent to the actors themselves . . . *habitus* is that part of practices which remain obscure in the eyes of their own producers' (Bourdieu 1977: 72–87).

Despite the fact that the people involved are not necessarily aware of what they are doing, in this view social agents are not objects guided by rules or codes. However, Bourdieu argues that social agents pursue strategies and weigh their 'interests' prior to any action. It is merely that these strategies are always in some way constrained by field and habitus.

Another of Bourdieu's key terms that seems particularly pertinent to the exploration of the formation of sensibilities about university choice and university prestige is his notion of '*doxa*', or the participant's 'commitment to the presuppositions' of the game that they are playing (Bourdieu 1990: 66), an 'undisputed, prereflexive, naïve, native compliance' (1990: 68) that gives us our 'feel' for what is, among other things, intuitively proper, fair, excellent or prestigious. Bourdieu adds that competitors in political power struggles often seek to appropriate 'the sayings of the tribe' (*doxa*) and thereby to appropriate 'the power the group exercises over itself' (1990: 110).

Even within the post-compulsory education system itself there are divisions and distinctions, which become apparent to those in the know. Competition for entry to the UK's more prestigious institutions and degree programmes has become increasingly fierce (Forsyth and Furlong 2000; Heath 2007). After university, competition is equally intense for the more highly prized graduate opportunities – the kinds of 'graduate jobs' that attract the high starting salaries (Brown and Hesketh 2004). Many researchers have drawn attention to the way that processes of exclusion still operate within elite higher education and the graduate labour market and how successful negotiation of these is often reliant upon the successful mobilization of economic, social and cultural resources in order to gain advantage within these competitive markets (Power *et al.* 2003; Ball *et al.* 2004; Brown *et al.* 2004; Brooks 2005; Reay *et al.* 2005; Heath 2007). This kind of literature makes extensive use of Bourdieu's work on forms of capital, in attempting to describe just what it is that makes certain youngsters more advantaged in this kind of competition for scarce places (Bourdieu 1986). In this literature, the concept of cultural capital helps researchers understand not only the ways in which cultural advantage and disadvantage are institutionalized through the acquisition of educational qualifications, but also the ways in which middle-class families are able to translate economic capital into forms of social and cultural capital to expedite their children's progress. In this way, 'social gifts' come to appear to be natural gifts (Bourdieu 1971), and middle-class educational and occupational proficiency is thus sustained and enhanced.

We have briefly reviewed these kinds of theories to show some of the diversity involved in thinking about the education system and how we might best understand what goes on there. Our thumbnail sketches would no doubt make most purists wince; however, the point is to show that the kinds of concepts and models we have to begin with help us look for particular kinds of phenomena in the educational arena. We might, for example, see the systems neatly interlocking and expediting the transition from childhood to adult concerns with work as per the functionalist model. More to the point, if youngsters are disruptive or challenging and more inclined to acquire an ASBO than an A level, this might be interpretable as a malfunction in the system rather than a failure on the part of parents, teachers or the teenagers themselves. Likewise, with Gadamer's picture of the educational process, this highlights the role of dialogue, discussion and mutuality in learning. Thus, this approach might lead us to highlight those meaningful conversations that occur out of formal classroom settings in transmitting the love of learning (Baker 2005). In the case of Bourdieu, we are given a variety of 'thinking tools' with which to explore how it is that the middle-class youngsters typically fare so well in education. Their advantage is far in excess of what we would expect simply by looking at their aptitude or IQ. By understanding their social positions as conferring different kinds of social or cultural capital, we can explain how some children seem to be perfectly matched to the education system whereas with others there always seems to be turbulence.

In the case of some approaches to knowledge, particularly those associated with the work of Karl Popper, the key element in research is testing hypotheses. An idea is developed and it is challenged against the data. The crucial thing is not to simply confirm it but to try to find evidence that will falsify it. The perspectives we have outlined above may appear disappointing from this point of view. They do not always readily yield testable hypotheses. We could never decisively falsify the intuition that people learn through conversation or decisively tell whether people have '*habitus*' or not.

Therefore, a theory in the social sciences – of which educational research is a part – does far more than generate testable hypotheses, though this is often an important function. To this function we can add several more functions or purposes of theory that social scientists have tried to identify over the last few decades. The sociologist Blumer (1970: 84) wrote:

> The point of developing theory is to outline and define life situations so that people may have a clearer understanding of their world through meaningful clarification of basic social values, modes of living and social relations.

Similarly, the anthropologist Geertz (1973: 5) offers the following:

> Believing, with Max Weber, that man (*sic*) is an animal suspended in webs of significance he himself has spun, I take culture to be those webs, and the analysis of it to be therefore not an experimental science in search of law but an interpretive one in search of meaning.
>
> Rather than seeking to develop theory in the form of a set of inter-related constructs. Theory as a *means of understanding* is often presented in the form of narratives (Coles 1989). Narrative is an integral way in which human intelligence organizes experience to grasp its meaning (Appleby *et al.* 1994). It often takes the form of what Buchannan (1998) calls 'a descriptive diagnosis of a situation'.

Theories also help to show how the social world is made up and how it is accomplished through the workings of the social actors in it. This kind of sense-making function of theory alludes to a particularly pervasive idea in the social sciences, namely the notion of the social construction of reality (Berger and Luckman 1966) or, as Searle (1995) rephrased it, the construction of social reality. Says Buchannan (1998: 245):

> Here, the contention is that, in the social world, the principles and values by which we lead our lives are not 'out there' embedded in the structure of the universe waiting to be discovered, but they are corrigible products of the human mind subject to constant revision and re-thinking.

Theories may thus go some way to showing us how the social world is made up. A further function of theory is to act as a sensitising perspective.

> The sensitizing function of theory serves to heighten people's awareness of a broader range of the particular contingencies bearing on a specific situation. Here, theory and research are used to sharpen, highlight and bring to the foreground as many aspects

> as possible that make the situation at hand unique, distinct and different from other situations. (Buchannan 1998: 446)

As well as sensitizing us to the unique features of the situation at hand, theories can also enable us to undertake a form of social critique. Much research in education is undertaken because researchers, educators or policy-makers want to make something better – to help students learn from feedback, to enable more people to benefit from a university education, to reduce 'social exclusion' and so on. Gitlin (1991) reminds us that a good deal of classical social theory in the nineteenth century was a kind of social critique, conceived in the hope of achieving some kind of social change. This can be traced back even earlier to the eighteenth-century Enlightenment, particularly where this was concerned with the problems resulting from existing power structures (Habermas 1988). Later in the nineteenth century, the works of Marx, Durkheim and Weber were all predicated on their authors' deep concern about the contemporary state of society.

The evidence-based agenda

As a number of observers (e.g. Evans and Benefield 2001) have pointed out, the twenty-first-century spirit in policy-making on the part of the UK Government has made research a key building block of its approach to policy. The use of research evidence in the formulation and evaluation of policy has become widespread across the range of public services. *Evidence-based* or *evidence-informed* policy and practice are politically modish. In the educational arena the twenty-first-century's spirit was captured by David Blunkett, who was the then Secretary of State for Education and Employment:

> Social science should be at the heart of policy-making. We need a revolution in relations between government and the social research community – we need social scientists to help to determine what

> works and why, and what types of policy initiatives are likely to be most effective. (DfEE 2000)

However, the question of what education is invites consideration of what knowledge is and what it does to human beings, and perhaps more pointedly, what a university is for. There have been a number of debates about what all this means in the context of a somewhat slippery notion that developed nations are now operating with 'knowledge economies' (Blackmore 2002). Debates about the changing nature of knowledge in the informational economy have been boiled down to four major perspectives on the future of the university (Delanty 2001: 149–50; Blackmore 2002) as:

1) **The entrenched liberal thesis** Here the university is seen as a site of cultural reproduction which needs to fend off challenges from political life and from those who would seek to dilute knowledge. For example, in the US especially, the traditional 'canon' of what is meant by great literature or significant science has been increasingly challenged by postmodernist and post-colonial scholars, who traditionalists are keen to fight off while they defend the traditional canon (Blackmore 2002).
2) **The postmodern thesis** Here, the end of the university is foreseen. Writers are apt to talk about the death of the author, the bankruptcy of established knowledges from the arts and sciences and the way that the university has lost its emancipatory role due to the fragmentation of knowledge and the separation of research from teaching (Lyotard 1984).
3) **The reflexivity thesis** This sees a new mode of knowledge emerging based on a reflexive relationship between users and producers of knowledge, as old forms of knowledge production are increasingly irrelevant to post-Fordist economies, e.g. Barnett (1997).
4) **The globalization thesis** This stresses the instrumentalization of the university as it embraces neoliberal market values and informational technology and becomes integrated into capitalist

> modes of production in developed economies. A new managerialist spirit facilitates capitalism's takeover but makes universities major players in the global information market and at the very heart of information-based capitalism (Rhoades and Slaughter 1998).

This rough sketch shows that different authors have highlighted some vastly different and contradictory pressures in universities, making it difficult to provide any sense of a unified purpose for universities and even less hope that they and their members will be singing from the same hymn sheet.

The question of research on higher education and the role of research on the higher educational process might be a little easier to do if we had some idea of what a university was for. As the comments above indicate, this is presently subject to a variety of different pressures. There have been a few scholars who over the years have tried to identify exactly what was special about a university. One of the most enduring and influential treatises on higher education has been John Henry Newman's *The idea of a university* (reprinted in Turner 1996). Although written and revised between 1852 and 1889, Newman's work has not lost its relevance with the passage of time (Craig *et al.* 1999). In Newman's view, an institution of higher learning is at its best when it's concerned with:

> . . . training good members of society. Its art is the art of social life, and its end is fitness for the world . . . a university training is the great ordinary means to a great but ordinary end; it aims at raising the intellectual tone of society, at cultivating the public mind, at purifying the national taste, at supplying true principles to popular enthusiasm and fixed aims to popular aspiration, at giving enlargement and sobriety to the ideas of the age, at facilitating the exercise of political power, and refining the intercourse of private life. It is the education which gives [a person] a clear, conscious view of their own opinions and judgements, a truth in developing them, an eloquence in expressing them, and a force in urging them.
>
> (Newman in Turner 1996: 125–6)

To some observers it would be desirable if educators in universities were to strive, like Socrates, to become 'by nature a disturber of the peace' (Passmore 1967: 203). But this particular goal would not be popular, and would be difficult to sustain in a contemporary 'corporate university'. Even in Passmore's day, at the cusp of the student unrest of the 1960s, he commented that: 'it is, indeed, by no means universally admitted that even at the University level students ought to be encouraged to think critically about the accepted beliefs and the accepted institutions of their communities . . .' (Passmore 1967: 203).

Kramnick (1997: 2) reinforced this line of thinking a little nearer the present in pointing out that in the contemporary world, the university is 'the only institution in our public life that is self-consciously skeptical, that questions, doubts or challenges the prevailing consensus on what is right, true, or good'.

As we shall see later, this scepticism and questioning is sometimes rather difficult to sustain in the current climate. For the moment, let us note that there are many commentators over the years who have identified a moral or aesthetic purpose to the institutions of higher education, as well as retaining the notion that those who work here must be able to 'speak truth to power'. That, however, is the story which people get out on special occasions. It is not so much that the present generation of scholars disagree with these sentiments, but that they have been occluded by mundane matters of 'key skills' and 'learning outcomes'.

The water is further muddied by concerns over what exactly the knowledge is that is being created and what it means. We shall discuss this question at greater length later in the book, but for the moment let us note that the issue of knowledge generation is by no means straightforward. From the 1970s to the present, a sub-discipline of sociology has been flourishing – concerned with how human beings collectively produce knowledge through professionalized scientific enquiry. One key figure here has been Bruno Latour, who, with Steve Woolgar, has produced a somewhat controversial picture of human enquiry in the sciences. They promote the notion that the objects of scientific study are *socially constructed* through the human process of discovery itself (Latour and Woolgar 1979). In other words, the phenomena we study cannot be presumed to exist with any certainty outside the instruments that measure them and the collective operation of the minds that interpret them. Latour would view scientific activity as a system of beliefs, oral traditions and culturally specific practices. In this view science is seen as a kind of culture. Not, as scientists themselves might have it, as a set of methodological principles (Latour 1987).

There are a number of other accounts of the process of discovering nature and representing it through scientific discourse which make similar points. Potter (1996) in his work on 'representing reality', or Bloor (1976) and his colleagues as part of the 'strong programme' in the sociology of science, have developed the notion that knowledge is sustained as much by the social and linguistic processes that go to make it up as by any simple correspondence to a reality 'out there' in nature.

This means that it is somewhat difficult to distil what it is that research in or on universities can contribute to a genuinely evidence-based practice in teaching and learning, when there is some uncertainty and instability about the nature of the knowledge we create. In the social sphere especially, claims that we are justified in making about what we know are more likely to be local rather than global, contingent rather than universal. This in turn means that policy-makers are apt to be frustrated when seeking guidance on what to do so as to better meet a politically desirable outcome.

How will policy-makers use evidence?

As many authors suggest (Nutley and Webb 2000; Evans and Benefield 2001), despite the occasional burst of enthusiasm on the part of politicians for social science research, policy-making is rarely a rational process, and evidence of 'what works' is only one consideration for policy-makers in their decision-making. Nutley and Webb (2000) and Weiss (1979) have tried to characterize the various ways in which policy-makers might use research evidence:

1) **The knowledge-driven model** This derives from the natural sciences. The fact that discoveries have been made sets up pressures for the development and use of the knowledge.
2) **The problem-solving model** This involves the direct application of the results of a specific study to an impending decision.
3) **The interactive model** Here, researchers are seen as one set of participants among many. The use of research forms part of a complicated process that might also depend upon experience, political insights and pressures, social technologies and guesswork.
4) **The political model** Here, research is used as political ammunition, especially where it is deployed to support a predetermined position.
5) **The tactical model** Research may be used as a delaying tactic in order to avoid taking responsibility for unpopular policies or potentially negative outcomes.
6) **The enlightenment model** This stresses the indirect influence of research rather than the direct impact of particular findings in the policy process. Thus the concepts and theoretical perspectives that social science engenders pervade the policy-making process.

This last point is perhaps the most telling. The economist John Maynard Keynes (1936: 393) summed up what he saw happening in the early years of the twentieth century:

> The ideas of economists and political philosophers, both when they are right and when they are wrong, are more powerful than is commonly understood. Indeed the world is ruled by little else. Practical men, who believe themselves to be quite exempt from any intellectual influence, are usually the slaves of some defunct economist. Madmen in authority, who hear voices in the air, are distilling their frenzy from some academic scribbler of a few years back.

The manifest position on evidence-based practice in education goes something like this: we all have a common goal of wanting to do our work in a way that is effective and efficient and brings desirable but cost-effective outcomes for students and teachers. The best way of establishing 'what works', presumably, is by experimentation (Evans and Benefield 2001). Based upon its success in medicine over the last 60 years, the kind of experimentation that has found particular favour is the randomized control trial. This is arguably better if we wish to identify causal relationships (Davies *et al.* 2000a). Indeed, the randomized controlled trial has been assigned such high status in this field that it has now come to define in American law what counts as 'rigorous' research and is the model of how evidence-based practice should be implemented (Feuer *et al.* 2002). The extent to which randomized controlled trials live up to their reputation in educational settings, however, is more debatable. Their detractors suggest that trials of this kind adopt a 'black box' model in which inferences are made not about innovations, but about a particular strategy for allocating subjects to experimental conditions. Thus, despite the claims made about them, they do not explain causes and instead simply offer pragmatic justifications (Davies *et al.* 2000b; Oliver and Conole 2003: 388).

The nature of evidence itself that goes to make up evidence-based or evidence-informed education is subject to careful selection by powerful people, deploying notions of scientific rigour borrowed from the natural sciences. In educational settings, the US government has thrown its weight behind evidence based on randomized controlled trials in evaluating educational interventions as these are believed to represent the best or 'gold standard' of scientific evidence (US Department of Education 2003). 'All evidence was not created equal' they counsel gravely. The kind of hierarchy of evidence one regularly sees in documents on both sides of the Atlantic is usually very similar to that provided in medicine by Sackett *et al.* (1996):

1 Strong evidence from at least one systematic review of multiple well-designed randomized controlled trials.
2 Strong evidence from at least one properly designed randomized controlled trial of appropriate size.

3 Evidence from well-designed trials such as non-randomized trials, cohort studies, time series or matched case-controlled studies.
4 Evidence from well-designed non-experimental studies from more than one centre or research group.
5 Opinions of respected authorities, based on clinical evidence, descriptive studies or reports of expert committees.

Thus, the only thing better than a randomized controlled trial is a large number of these which are sufficiently similar that their data (or perhaps some measure of effect size) can be added together in a meta analysis or systematic review. This then is the evidence on which practitioners are encouraged to base their work. The spectacle of ineffective *shibboleths* falling before the astute scrutiny of scientifically trained researchers is sometimes an attractive one and the appeal of the evidence-based bandwagon is sufficient that most of those hale and hearty enough are attempting to climb aboard it.

As Traynor (2000) notes, the movement has a curious taint of stridency, and the reader is often urged, as in US Department of Education documents, to observe a strict diet and eschew any research that does not meet the most stringent quality standards – in other words, anything which is not a randomized controlled trial. In education in the UK, as Hammersley (2001) reminds us, the appeal of systematic reviews has recently gained considerable ground. Such reviews, it is hoped, will play an important part in making research evidence available in a usable form to policy-makers and practitioners, and we shall explore whether they could ever live up to their promise in Chapter 6.

This tendency, however, is certainly one that attracts criticism. As well as doubts as to whether it genuinely penetrates to the causes of phenomena in the social world, there are concerns about the political imperatives that seem to be bound up in the evidence-based movement. The 'gold standard' of randomized controlled trials and systematic reviews is argued by Nespor (2006) to be part of a larger agenda that involves more than epistemology and methodology, and is part of a more systematic effort to ontologically standardize the educational system (Espeland and Stevens 1998). This standardization approach also makes a number of assumptions regarding the things we are studying. For example, imagining that they are readily definable in terms which we can agree upon, that they can easily be measured and that the measurements can be agreed upon, and that suitable outcomes can also be agreed as desirable and the measurement of these can be undertaken with similar agreement. A moment's reflection tells us that many educational phenomena, such as good teaching and good learning, and desirable outcomes such as critical thinking, happiness, quality of life or human well-being can be very difficult to define, despite the large number of self-report questionnaires which claim to measure them.

The gold standard approach also leaves unexamined another field of phenomena. Some authors (Bowker and Star 1999; Nespor 2006) have suggested that, by analogy with 'structural violence' or 'structural racism' when we look at human-service organizations, they have a large-scale ecology that gives rise to a set of 'structural methods' or methodological 'infrastructures' which enable them to do their ontological construction work. That is, they are often hard at work shaping categories and identities, building material and social environments, and so forth. People and organizations move artefacts and representations around and animate knowledge-constitutive networks. In other words, they do the work needed to constitute the object of our enquiry in the first place – the 'minority student', the 'learning outcome' or the 'assessment criteria' are seldom natural kinds – they take quite a lot of collective work to build them in the first place. Likewise, 'the classroom', 'the seminar group' or even 'the university' all were constructed through assiduous human activity. Therefore, some commentators such as Nespor (2006) are sceptical of the value of including things that are human constructions as if they were variables in experiments. That leaves out a lot of the more troubling epistemological fabric of the world.

A further assumption of this model of evidence-based practice is that the local relevance of findings deduced from 'gold standard' studies is self-evident. They will simply tell you what works best and require little or no expert mediation. As one US summary puts it: 'a key virtue of the randomized experiment' is that 'there is much less controversy about what the finding is . . . randomized experiments increase the probability of the use of research results compared with other forms of research' (Brookings Institution 1999).

Nevertheless, despite these concerns, there have been some influential calls for the adoption of a rigorous evidence-based approach to practice in education. Sometimes this comes from funding bodies such as the Economic and Social Research Council in the UK. Its Teaching and Learning Research Programme was designed to support programmes of research with a 'practical focus' as Grenfell and James (2004) note, combined with a strong steer towards randomized controlled trials.

The UK's Higher Education Academy is keen to promote dialogue concerning what evidence-based practice might mean in education. Their manifesto is founded on the assumption that if staff who work in universities are to improve their practice as teachers, managers, administrators or service providers, and if they are to be better able to adapt to continuous and complex change, then they will need to better understand and use evidence so as to inform decisions about change and how, when and why evidence-based change should be implemented.

This invites the question of what sort of evidence our plans for educational change must be based upon. In the view of some commentators it is not particularly promising. In 1996, David Hargreaves delivered an influential speech at the UK's Teacher Training Agency, in which he argued that educational research had lost its way, was remote from practice, of poor quality and a waste of public money. Hargreaves (1997: 413) argues that: 'research should provide decisive and conclusive evidence that if teachers do X rather than Y in their professional practice, there will be a significant and enduring improvement in outcome'.

The list of criticisms laid at the door of educational research is a long one, and includes such gross moral turpitude as lack of rigour; failure to produce cumulative research findings; theoretical incoherence; ideological bias; irrelevance to the needs of educational institutions; lack of involvement of practitioners; that it is inaccessible and poorly disseminated, and that it is not cost-effective (Whitty 2006: 161).

A similar exhortation towards more practically instrumental research was apparent in the first consultation paper produced by the National Educational Research Forum (NERF 2000), which was taken to be promoting a somewhat limited and overly positivistic view of research. The fact that this kind of research was being promoted by a national body was seen as highly sinister by Stephen Ball, who responded that it treated research as if it were 'about providing accounts of what works for unselfconscious classroom drones to implement' and that it portended 'an absolute standardization of research purposes, procedures, reporting and dissemination' (Ball 2001: 266–7).

Grenfell and James (2004) argue that these developments themselves can be understood in terms of Bourdieu's theory. Policy-makers, funding bodies and professional organizations are trying to exert influence so as to change a field of knowledge. They are trying to do so by means of the imposition of criteria of legitimacy and the reformulation of institutional relations and structures – the research councils in the UK are keen to see 'end-user involvement' specified in research proposals. The capital value of research activity is redefined and its currency values are altered. With the changes in funding patterns come changes in knowledge itself, and there are consequent gains and losses in power and influence. Nothing is as good for one's career in research as the landing of a handsome research grant, and nothing so likely to ensure that one will get another in the future. This itself changes the fabric (or in Bourdieu's terms the 'field') of what is known and what can be known in the future.

Despite the enthusiasm with which it has been embraced in some quarters, the evidence-based or evidence-informed agenda has not permeated all aspects of education. As Deem (2006) points out, managers are often relatively untouched by these imperatives. Despite the popularity of evidence-based practice in education and related public-service disciplines' evidence-based practice, its stipulations have been applied largely to the process of teaching and learning and there is little indication that this debate has 'significantly permeated HE management *qua* management' (Deem 2006: 204).

Participating as a researcher in the evidence-based agenda is sometimes far from straightforward either. There is a strong suspicion among many researchers that if one's research is not supportive of government policy then there can be major difficulties (Baty and Shepherd 2006). Researchers whose work has yielded findings that do not accord with government policy in high-profile contexts claim to have been subject to 'concerted campaigns of vilification, have had their work publicly rubbished and have been subjected to repeated personal criticisms'. Peter Tymms, of Durham University, controversially reported that in a study of 20,000 11-year-old children, those who did the most homework performed the least well on tests. Subsequently, David Blunkett, when he was the Secretary of State for Education said that no-one with 'the slightest common sense' could possibly take the research seriously. Tymms, a Professor of Education at the University of Durham, was one of those academics who is 'so out of touch' that they 'churn out' irrelevant findings that should be ignored (Shepherd 2006).

Conclusion: towards evidence-informed heresy

In this introductory chapter we have aimed to give the reader a brief tour of some of the issues with which we will be concerned in this book. There are a variety of strands to this scholarship and by way of conclusion we would like to draw attention to some themes and issues which will return to the surface of our thinking as we traverse the following chapters.

One important theme which we want the reader to bear in mind is that there are many different ways of looking at things. The positions we take towards science and knowledge are often just provisional standpoints among myriad different means of grasping what is going on in higher education or anywhere else.

This is not to say it is 'all about perspective' or 'all about context' in any simple sense. Human ways of knowing can take on a solidity and durability that can sustain them through many centuries of social change as the context around them changes dramatically.

It is also important to think about knowledge and how human beings acquire it with the benefit of history. Forms of human enquiry have not always looked like they do now, and it is likely that they will change again within our lifetimes. Randomized controlled trials are thought of as a medical activity, but in medicine they emerged fairly recently and are a post-World War II invention. The procedures we follow to find out about the educational world are not just simply there as aspects of the scientific bedrock. They came to look like they do now as a result of discussion, conflict and struggle. In some cases, the conflict is far from over.

We want to be able to explore the emphasis on research in higher education in a number of directions. We will be asking how it originated and what philosophical assumptions it brings with it. We will be asking about the extent to which the present form in which it is manifest will reproduce existing power structures and give support to political regimes which have already taken their decisions and made their commitments.

We will also be asking about the kind of knowledge we have about universities and what this knowledge represents. To what extent can knowledge be said to be conjured up through everyday social practices? Or is it, in best positivist spirit, derived from what is out there in nature? Come to think of it, is this what positivism was really about in the first place?

This last question segues neatly into Chapter 2. The truth is out there.

2

The truth is out there? Positivism and realism

Introduction

The terms positivism and realism are familiar to anyone who has read about the philosophy of science, yet we need to clarify what these traditions contribute to current thinking. In this chapter, we will survey what these forms of thinking have contributed to educational matters and what they have added to our understanding of research processes.

Research could be described as a systematic investigation (Burns 1997) or form of inquiry that involves the collection of data, its analysis and interpretation, in an effort to 'understand, describe, predict or control an educational or psychological phenomenon or to empower individuals in such contexts' (Mertens 2005: 2). A number of commentators (O'Leary 2004; Mackenzie and Knipe 2006) have described how the process of human enquiry in the educational field, which seemed relatively simple to define a generation ago, has become far more complex in recent times, with the number of possible research methods increasing dramatically, 'particularly in the social/applied sciences' (O'Leary 2004: 8). In the field of qualitative inquiry especially, there has been a frenetic jostling of different brands with seductive titles like 'phenomenography', 'interpretive phenomenological analysis' and 'discursive hermeneutic analysis'. Quantitative research, too, has been transformed by the desire of researchers to incorporate explorations of multiple variables through increasingly complex regression and structural equation modelling techniques. We will describe some of these later, but for the moment let us merely note that there has been a proliferation of different research techniques. In many parts of the world, the journey of doctoral students has been increasingly one of becoming familiar with the sheer range of research techniques as well as completing a thesis.

To complicate matters even further, it is suggested that the 'exact nature of the definition of research is influenced by the researcher's theoretical framework' (Mertens 2005: 2), where there can even be some grey areas as to what counts as research. Is an activity with researchers an 'audit', or is it 'continuing professional development' or is it genuine 'research'? Elliott (2006) describes how, early in his career, he was involved in some work with teachers that had them working together to develop solutions to problems they had identified. This, his senior colleagues told him, was continuing professional development rather than real 'research'.

In a good deal of research, the problem, question or hypothesis that the researchers are investigating is informed by theory, which gives them a suspicion that there may be relationships between, or among, constructs that describe or explain a phenomenon. The thing about theory is that it enables the researcher to 'go beyond' the local event and enables them to connect it with similar events (Mertens 2005: 2).

This chapter will get us started in the philosophy of science proper. That is, we will deal with one of the standard set pieces of the philosophy of science, namely positivism. The persistence of positivism in books about the philosophy of science is peculiar, in that it flourished relatively briefly in the nineteenth century and again in the early twentieth and hardly anyone today would admit to being a positivist. Indeed, it is a kind of insult in the present day, being used largely to describe work one does not like, especially if it is considered to be particularly mindless and inhumane. Indeed, positivism is increasingly excluded from attempts to philosophize about education. However, the impact of positivism on the shaping of modern scientific enquiry and scientific attitudes has been profound. Most alternative philosophies of science have originated as a kind of dialogue with what their makers thought of as positivism, or as an attempt to clarify, extend or transcend positivism.

Positivism: The facts that began to speak for themselves

We will begin our story with positivism itself. The basic idea – that it was possible to develop knowledge systems which avoided theology, speculation and metaphysics, and which rely exclusively on what can be observed – was most thoroughly developed in the mid-nineteenth century work of Auguste Comte (1798–1857). Even so, Comte's dream of a positive philosophy based on observation which would liberate humanity from the failures of tradition was only one of a number of important but lesser known strands in nineteenth-century thinking.

Positivism was a theory of knowledge; a theory about the evolution of human societies and formed a set of recommendations for carrying out inquiry. According to Comte, societies must universally undergo three distinct phases in their quest for knowledge. These are the theological, the metaphysical and the positive phases.

The theological phase of human evolution, which Comte also called the 'fictitious' phase, is characterized by the belief that the world is infused with magical, spiritual or theological phenomena. Tales were reaching Europe concerning the belief systems of people in far-flung parts of the European nations' empires, and these invariably involved a rich array of invisible beings whose actions propelled physical and human phenomena. In Europe itself, from the beginning of Christianity until the Renaissance, intellectual life was based on a whole-hearted belief that all things had reference to God. The place of human beings in society and the wider natural world was governed by their association with the divine presences and with the Church that governed all. The theological phase therefore involves humankind, despite disputes and heresies, broadly accepting the notion of gods, and eventually a single God, and accepting religious authority from the Church.

Comte describes the metaphysical phase in the evolution of human thought as one where people seek knowledge of the unifying principles of nature rather than God. This characteristic is present in human enquiry in Europe from the Renaissance, through eighteenth-century enlightenment and into the nineteenth century. It was a time when logical rationalism gained a progressively greater hold over the imaginations of intellectuals. It also corresponded to a growing concern with universal 'rights of man' and the idea that 'man', (with a very few exceptions, writers were not overly concerned with what happened to women), is born with certain rights, that cannot be taken away, which must be respected.

The final stage of Comte's universal law of development is the scientific or positive stage. This stage contains a number of ideas that inform both politics and human enquiry. Politically, the central idea of this phase is that individual rights are more important than the rule of any one person. This stage is intrinsically different from the others in the idea that man (*sic*) is able to govern himself. In science, Comte believed that each field of study had attained the positive level at a different time. Comte ranked mathematics first (as the most general and independent), then astronomy, physics, chemistry, biology and, finally, sociology – the 'queen of the sciences'. The latter, truly a science of society, was the last to attain the positive method. This method involves assigning priority to sensory data.

> All competent thinkers agree with Bacon that there can be no real knowledge except that which rests upon observed facts. This fundamental maxim is evidently indisputable if it is applied, as it ought to be, to the mature state of our intelligence.
>
> (Comte 1976/1851: 3)

Positivism was popularized in the Anglophone world, especially by John Stuart Mill (1882). His interest in evolutionary stages chimed in with a great deal of the work of nineteenth-century intellectuals as they struggled with the problems of interpreting nature and human society in physical terms, without reference to any divine or natural vitalistic force of nature. Karl Marx, Herbert Spencer and, of course, Darwin himself were preoccupied with evolutionary change; they and many other thinkers saw their work as part of a single intellectual endeavour geared towards unity in knowledge. This is not to say that they all agreed, or cited each others' work approvingly, but rather that there was a thematic consistency in the way that these thinkers addressed the problem of knowledge and sought to apply it to the explanation and improvement of society.

Most importantly from our point of view, as the nineteenth century progressed, there was a concern to understand societal phenomena. Brown *et al.* (2003) foregrounded the work of Comte's near contemporary Lambert Adolphe Quetelet (1796–1874), as one of the first to introduce statistical methods into the human sciences. Quetelet became fascinated by tables of mortality rates, crime rates and illnesses, such as were newly available from the governments of Europe. Rates of crime, illness and death obeyed a curious stability from one year to the next which puzzled intellectuals of the day – surely the decision to commit murder, perpetrate a robbery, or whether one succumbed to illness was a profoundly individual matter? The discovery of these regularities was a source of great excitement to Quetelet, who believed they would reveal information of great importance to entrepreneurs and governments (Murphy and Cooper 2000). He called this new science social mechanics.

Quetelet was also one of the first to borrow probabilistic notions and import them into this new science of social mechanics. In particular, the idea of a normal distribution, first invented in 1733 by DeMoivre and popularized by Gauss in 1809 to describe the pattern of error in astronomical measurement, could, Quetelet discovered, describe the pattern of variability in measurements of human characteristics and human activity. All of a sudden, the human sciences had become statistical disciplines (Hankins 1968, originally published in 1908). This tradition was, of course, carried forward with the attempts by Emile Durkheim to use suicide rates to specify the kind of society and social matrix within which the suicides take place. The measurement and systematic comparison of people and their characteristics led, through the work of Francis Galton, to the development of twentieth-century educational psychology. One of the important features of Quetelet's thinking was that facts could 'speak for themselves', or rather 'speak loudly of their own accord'. As well as pushing statistical techniques into the human and moral disciplines, Quetelet made the fact–value distinction a central feature of his new social mechanics – the idea that it was possible to have knowledge, especially of a quantitative kind, from which morality and values had been excluded.

Positivism provided a rationale for the shifts in patterns of knowing, types of knowledge, and the development of knowledge in the nineteenth and early twentieth centuries and provided a protocol for the way in which this new-found knowledge should impact on practice, policy and education. Auguste Comte's vision of sociologists as a new priestly caste – he even designed them costumes – may seem amusing, but it reflects a much more durable idea that social problems could be addressed via research, which has left its imprint on present-day approaches to human welfare, such as the vogue at the time of writing for so-called 'evidence-based practice'.

Education: Measuring, defining and diagnosing

In England toward the end of the nineteenth century, the question of education for children who appeared unable to benefit from the mass elementary education introduced by the 1870 Elementary Education Act soon began to exercise experts (Read and Walmsley 2006). A band of often 'undernourished, unwell, unclad, filthy, exhausted and disabled children' (Potts 1983: 182) were falling behind in the academic curriculum of the classes in elementary schools. The first Local Authority employed educational psychologist Cyril Burt, who, speaking towards the end of his life, characterized the situation at the end of the nineteenth century:

> The older voluntary schools had been able to refuse the duller and the more troublesome youngsters if they wished. Consequently the newer school boards were obliged to accept the rejects. As a result, their classrooms we are told were often crammed with an aggregation of difficult children; urchins who could not be taught, ruffians who could not be controlled, and the protests of the teachers emphasized the need for a systematic investigation into the whole of the problems thus created. Accordingly, during the next two or

> three decades, inquiries were started by several independent bodies. (quoted in Rushton 2002: 559)

By the end of the nineteenth century the idea was firmly entrenched that the social difficulties in the education system and elsewhere could be addressed via the systematic investigation of the phenomenon in question. Charles Booth investigated poverty, crime and mortality rates. Francis Galton had great faith in measuring people, at the Great Exhibition, at the London Science Museum and at University College. Some of his posters survive:

> A Laboratory has now been instituted for the measurement of form and faculty, partly for experiment and research, partly to familiarize the public with the uses of human measurement. By this means, you may learn something of your own bodily and mental powers and those of your children and so gain timely warning of remedial faults or defects in their development. Charge, three pence to those on the register, four pence to those who are not.

From the point of view of education however, the key question was how to measure the mental characteristics as well as the physical ones. Thresholds of sensation, reaction times and just noticeable differences between phenomena offered some hope, but what was urgently desired was a means of differentiating between pupils in terms of their likely educational prowess. The early results were not promising. The various measures of sensory discrimination, memory, reaction time, sensitivity to pain, puzzle-solving and all the other 'mental tests' hitherto devised did not all point in the same direction. Surveying the field in 1904, Charles Spearman's account conveys the frustration:

> Thus far, it must be confessed, the outlook is anything but cheerful for our project contemplated . . . There is scarcely one positive conclusion concerning the correlation between mental tests and independent practical estimates that has not been with equal force flatly contradicted; and amid this discordance, there is a continually

> waxing inclination – especially noticeable among the most capable workers and exact results – absolutely to deny any such correlation at all. (Spearman 1904: 219)

Spearman's solution was to focus the field in upon a much smaller set of activities whose results did tend to correlate together. The alacrity with which the people tested solved various mental puzzle-type items (looking remarkably similar to contemporary intelligence test items), seemed to correlate together and, more to the point, corresponded to their ability to do well in the education system. Thus, Spearman pared away all the things that did not correlate with this – the sensory thresholds, the reaction times and the physical measurements. At the same time, of course, there were developments in France by Binet and Simon to identify 'new methods for the diagnosis of the intellectual level of subnormals' (Binet 1905). Through psychometric testing, the subnormal child could be identified and diagnosed by analogy with medical diagnosis.

The late nineteenth and early twentieth centuries also saw a growth in the separatist model of education for children who were judged to be problematic within the mainstream system. Once it was possible for the children to be identified through a systematic and scientific procedure it would be possible to segregate them into the recently established 'special schools'. These were considered models of practice to be emulated and accounts of their workings were published by the School Board, and by commentators such as Morley (1897) and Philpott (1904), who both identified the need to focus on each child. Aside from their segregation at school, it was envisaged that the children would live within the community. Morley's account of a south-east London Special School concludes with the following passage:

> Picture the poor dullards in the old unenlightened days – locked up in lonely rooms, perhaps crouching in corners, turned out into the streets, the sullen, the mischievous, the stupid, the inarticulate – with asylum or workhouse surely looming in the distance. Picture them now! (Morley 1897: 174–75)

The enlightened identification, diagnosis and special education of dullards was often believed to be considerably better than the neglect or harsh treatment they might have previously received. The educational measurement of children and the scientific identification of feeble-mindedness, the creation of educational experiences suited to them, the rational planning of society – all these were grist to the positivists' mill.

But there was more. Once it became possible to measure children and adults in this way, it became possible to discover new concerns. The interior territory of the developing mind was thrown open to the clear light of psychological scrutiny. It became apparent that feeble-mindedness was far more widespread than had hitherto been suspected. Even worse, those who were apt to delinquency, drunkenness or licentiousness were disproportionately likely to score low on tests of cognitive ability or mental age. Lewis Terman, a leading advocate of intelligence testing in the US, was able to answer the question with some degree of assurance:

> But why do the feeble-minded tend so strongly to become delinquent? The answer may be stated in simple terms. Morality depends upon two things: (a) the ability to foresee and to weigh the possible consequences for self and others of different kinds of behaviour; and (b) upon the willingness and capacity to exercise self-restraint. That there are many intelligent criminals is due to the fact that (a) may exist without (b). On the other hand, (b) presupposes (a). In other words, not all criminals are feeble-minded, but all feeble-minded are at least potential criminals. That every feeble-minded woman is a potential prostitute would hardly be disputed by any one. Moral judgment, like business judgment, social judgment, or any other kind of higher thought process, is a function of intelligence. Morality cannot flower and fruit if intelligence remains infantile. (Terman 1916: 9)

This desire to know, to measure and to classify and determine policy accordingly has been with us in the educational field ever since. The technologies of measurement are combined in rather heady ways with the values of the age. The distinction between facts and values insisted upon by the likes of Quetelet and Comte did not necessarily lead to an ideologically pure science but instead allowed the mores of the time to be cloaked in science. What is touted as rational, enlightened practice a century ago looks instead by the standards of our own time to be bordering upon barbarism. Now this is not to say that the practitioners and researchers of the time were antediluvian brutes or misogynists. This simply shows how vastly different thinking and social practice were a century ago.

Nevertheless, there are curious resonances with the present in the UK. Admission to popular universities which attract most applicants is becoming problematic because of the sheer number of applicants now gaining 'A' and 'B' grades at A level. Some schools, notably those in the private sector, are intending to offer more demanding qualifications so that supposedly more able youngsters will have more impressive qualifications with which to impress admissions tutors at elite universities. The 'pre U' qualification and a variant of the American Scholastic Aptitude Tests are under discussion, as well as the International Baccalaureate (Griffith 2006). These, it is argued, will stretch out the distribution of scores among the most 'able' applicants. Like the intelligence tests in the early years of the twentieth century, there might equally be a suspicion that what is being tested is at least in part the cultural capital available to certain children by virtue of their parents' wealth or expertise.

Positivism peters out: The fall from grace

By the middle years of the twentieth century the key features of positivism, as presented by Hacking (1981), had condensed into the following set of propositions:

1) A focus on science as a product, a linguistic or numerical set of statements.
2) A concern with axiomatization, that is, with demonstrating the logical structure and coherence of these statements.

3) An insistence on at least some of these statements being testable, that is amenable to being verified, confirmed or falsified by the empirical observation of reality; statements that would, by their nature, be regarded as untestable included the teleological – the concerns with ends – and thus attempts to eliminate classical metaphysics.
4) The belief that science is markedly cumulative.
5) The belief that science is predominantly transcultural.
6) The belief that science rests on specific results that are dissociated from the personality and social position of the investigator.
7) The belief that science contains theories or research traditions that are largely commensurable.
8) The belief that science sometimes incorporates new ideas that are discontinuous from old ones.
9) The belief that science involves the idea of the unity of science, that there is, underlying the various scientific disciplines, basically one science about one real world.

Positivism is also associated with the belief that real knowledge is scientific, and that the phenomena worth knowing about are ultimately measurable. Positivism is also associated with reductionism, in that it is believed that entities of one kind can be reduced to entities of another kind for explanatory purposes. Thus, societies can be reduced to numbers, mental events can be reduced to neurological events and these can be reduced to chemical events and so on. From the point of view of the social scientist, social processes are reducible to relationships between and actions of individuals and biological organisms can be reduced and explained in terms of physical systems.

Positivism is out of favour in educational research at present. Despite the exhortations towards research based upon randomized controlled trials coming from government circles on both sides of the Atlantic, educational researchers and those whose job it is to teach students about scientific research methods are often hostile towards the movement.

The term 'positivist' has become a term of abuse, and is pretty much the worst thing that could be said about a philosopher or social scientist. Indeed, once a particular piece of research is described as 'positivist', then that is more or less the end of the discussion. 'It is difficult to think of any term in the educational lexicon so laden with negative connotations as "positivism"' (Matthews 2004: 7).

Positivism is seen as the worm in the bud of human enquiry, and its contamination is thought to go back a long way. Perhaps it is possible to locate the beginning of the malaise in the Enlightenment because 'technical rationality underpins the *myth of positivism* that enshrined the empirical-analytic sciences as the source of secure and privileged knowledge of the world' (Milne and Taylor 1998: 28). The Enlightenment was a time when 'technical rationality gained an exalted status . . . and colonized the social sciences and, later, education as they were admitted to the university' (Milne and Taylor 1998:28).

Henry Giroux, a longstanding critic of corporate influence and neoliberal ideologies in education maintains that the culture of positivism has become a dominant ideology and 'now represents an integral part of the social and political system of the United States' (Giroux 1981: 42). As well as policy, positivism is also believed to be responsible for corrupting scientific enquiry itself: 'the other major failing of science . . . is its positivist-reductionist nature' (Cross and Price 1992: 7). Its lingering legacy has been detected in the social sciences also. Sandra Harding notes that although there are not many scientists, social scientists and philosophers calling themselves 'positivists', 'most of these people still happily embrace fundamental assumptions of positivism' (Harding 1991: 79).

Positivism is not only charged with having distorted science and the practice of education, but Matthews (2004: 9) alleged it to be responsible for having misdirected educational research as a whole. The contributions to Gage's *Handbook of Research on Teaching* (Gage 1963) and Travers' *Second Handbook of Research on Teaching* (Travers 1973) are regarded as exemplars of the 'continued allegiance of educational research to logical positivism' (Munby and Russell 1998: 646). The ire of many researchers in the US has been raised by the ghost of positivism haunting the role of educational research, described in the recently enacted US

Federal Bill 'No Child Left Behind' (2001). Here it is stipulated that federal research funds are to be used only to support 'scientifically based research'; where such research is defined as 'rigorous, systematic and objective procedures to obtain valid knowledge', and where the research 'is evaluated using experimental or quasi-experimental designs' (Slavin 2002: 15).

Positivists were the first postmodernists

The situation with regard to positivism is complicated, however. Despite the confidence with which many writers dismiss positivism, it is hard to reconcile what they think it is with what people involved with the movement were actually doing or saying. Many of the charges tendered by contemporary authors about what positivism was and what it involved are not borne out by careful study of what positivism was about. The story of positivism did not stop with the end of the nineteenth century because the ideas within this influential way of looking at the relationship between science, society and the natural world were very attractive to a number of later European thinkers. In the early years of the twentieth century positivism was dominated by the Vienna Circle. A group of scholars from the University of Vienna began to meet to discuss ideas about science, from about 1907 onwards. They included Otto Neurath, a sociologist, Hans Hahn, a mathematician, and Philipp Frank, a physicist. Later, in the 1920s, Moritz Schlick became the leader and arranged for Rudolf Carnap to join them in 1926. The so-called Vienna Circle ceased to function as a coherent group in the 1930s with the rise of Nazism, especially as many of its members were Jewish or had Marxist sympathies, or both. Their leader, Moritz Schlick, was shot and killed on the steps of the main university building by one of his students in 1936 (Sarkar 1996). The progressive Marxist orientation contrasts oddly with the subsequent idea that positivism leads to socially retrogressive policies. The idea that truth could set humanity free from centuries of tradition and oppression was at the time an idea of the Vienna Circle, a central part of positivist doctrine. The Vienna Circle's collectively written manifesto 'The Scientific World-Conception: The Vienna Circle' concluded with the sentence 'The scientific world-conception serves life, and life receives it' (Carnap *et al.* 1973: 318). They were akin to an 'International Liberation Front', albeit of an intellectual and cultural kind (Toulmin 1969: 51).

Although they are thought of mainly for their contributions to the philosophy of science, in the form of 'logical positivism', the Vienna Circle members were also especially interested in language, and were concerned with how we could know the truth about statements which were made about the world. Their overarching concern was with verification. A statement was meaningful insofar as it could be challenged against facts which might verify or refute it. Probably most Vienna Circle members would have concurred with Carnap's idea that the essential problem faced by the scientist was to do with verifying statements about the world with immediately given sense data. In his 1928 *magnum opus* 'The logical structure of the world', Carnap argued that all terms suited to describe empirical facts are definable in terms referring exclusively to elements of immediate experience (Sarkar 1996).

The assumption that positivism involves a belief in an external world is also not borne out by the later writings of the Vienna Circle, whose radical empiricism led them to doubt that we could ever know anything about the would outside our heads for certain. Some of its members and many subsequent thinkers were led away from a foundationalist model of scientific enquiry altogether (Uebel 1996). Some, especially Otto Neurath, were increasingly preoccupied with the difficulty of making any statements about the world. He described scientific enquiry in the following terms: 'We are like sailors who have to rebuild their ship on the open sea, without ever being able to dismantle it in drydock and reconstruct it from the best components.' This formulation of the task of knowing has been adopted also by Ayer (1959) and Quine (1990). It graphically depicts the anti-*foundationalism* Neurath ended up with as he followed a strong empirical position of doubting everything. This doubt extended beyond epistemology and included the social sciences, society and politics: knowledge and life are built without foundations. In tandem with this,

Neurath pushed positivism away from ideas about truth or verification based on sensory experience, but toward the coherence of our statements. In this way, his work had parallels with Wittgenstein's focus on language. Thus he set the stage for more explicitly anti-foundationalist philosophies which we shall review in detail later. Following on from the ideas expressed in Neurath's boat analogy, Rorty (1979) expressed profound scepticism that it would ever be possible to judge the truth of our beliefs from an objective or transcendental standpoint.

The legacy of positivism is thus rather difficult to come to terms with in educational research. It is at present in a curious limnal state, at once reviled and at the same time subject to some rehabilitation, in that people have started to look at it again more sympathetically. As Friedman (1999: xv) says:

> As scholarly investigations of the past fifteen or twenty years into the origins of logical empiricism have increasingly revealed, such a simple-minded radically empiricist picture of this movement is seriously distorted. Our understanding of logical positivism and its intellectual significance must be fundamentally revised when we reinsert the positivists into their original intellectual context, that of the revolutionary scientific developments, together with the equally revolutionary philosophical developments, of their time. As a result, our understanding of the significance of the rise and fall of logical positivism for our own time also must be fundamentally revised.

The purpose here is not to deny that educational phenomena are researchable, but to highlight for the reader how tenuous and fragile that knowledge is and to make explicit the assumptions upon which it rests. In the same way, the early promise of reductionism has progressively been eroded through the twentieth century through a profound uncertainty with the nature of matter, space and time.

A somewhat more nuanced account of positivism's surviving principles in the late-twentieth century is provided by Nussbaum (Nussbaum 1990, Elliott 2006). Positivism, as Comte and the Vienna Circle advocated, links theory and practice in terms of a logic that sutures an objectivist view of knowledge to an instrumentalist view of practical reason. These links involve what Nussbaum (1990: 56–7) calls 'the science of measurement'. She believes that this 'scientific' conception of rationality involves four major constitutive claims that are still apparent in contemporary social science.

1) The claim of 'metricity' which assumes that 'in a particular choice situation there is some one value, varying only in quantity, that is common to all the alternatives'. Under this logic, the rational chooser will use this single standard as a metric to weigh each alternative and determine which will yield the greatest value.
2) The claim of 'singularity', which involves the contention that one and the same metric or standard applies in all situations of choice.
3) The claim of 'consequentialism', to the effect that the chosen actions have instrumental value as a means of producing good consequences.
4) By combining each of these claims we have the principle of 'maximization' which is 'that there is some one value, that it is the point of rational choice, in every case, to maximize'.

This, roughly, is the position where formulating evidence-based policy is concerned. The overt position of policy-making and research in education has been shaped by this self-consciously 'scientific' picture of practical reasoning (Elliott and Doherty 2001: 209–21, Schwandt 2005: 294–95, Elliott 2006). In this way, the educational reforms initiated by many governments are viewed as devices for 'driving up standards', 'widening participation' and so on, conceived of in terms of metricity and singularity.

Metricity and singularity in educational research – but what on earth are we measuring?

In this climate, research is geared towards evaluating the effectiveness of schools, teachers, techniques and programmes aimed at determining how schools, teachers and initiatives can 'add value' to students' learning and increase their propensity to enter university. For example, towards the end of 2006, the UK's Higher Education Funding Council for England (HEFCE 2006) published a report concerned with the effectiveness of widening participation initiatives. This suggested that there was strong evidence that the widening participation activities of institutions and government-backed initiatives such as the UK's 'Aimhigher' were helping to raise the aspirations of people in target groups. But evidence is weak of any positive impact on widening access to higher education or the attainment levels of the target groups (Tysome 2006). This concern is reinforced by a publication from the Department for Education and Skills (DfES 2006) which suggests that while progress has been made in broadening the socio-economic make-up of the higher education student population, this has been 'too slow' and may be levelling off. This chimes in with suggestions on the basis of a survey of social mobility in the UK compared with other countries, that the likelihood of social mobility in the UK is becoming less over time because, as the authors put it, increased opportunities to stay on in the education system at 16 and 18 are disproportionately benefiting the middle classes (Blandon *et al.* 2005). To add to the complications, it is not clear whether the budget addressing widening participation issues is effective because it has not been possible to disaggregate it from the rest of the money spent by HEFCE via the universities.

Now if we were to take Nussbaum's formulation of the process in a strong form, we would expect to see the maximization principle embedded in the idea of 'value added', which presumes that the practices of universities, schools, teachers, lecturers and administrators have value, and have spent the money wisely if they produce good consequences and that these should be quantifiable in terms of a single metric that applies generally across the system. As we can see here, the policies do not appear to be working as the government intended and it has not been possible to keep track of the money in any meaningful way. This means that despite a vast amount of effort and money devoted to the research in question, the evidence-based practice model advocated cannot be implemented meaningfully.

One of the problems in trying to apply this kind of model to doing research on the higher education enterprise is that many of its constructs do not necessarily resolve themselves neatly into things that we can operationalize and measure. Despite massive investments in the assurance and measurement of quality in higher education around the world and a journal devoted to it, it is still hard to achieve a precise definition. Some authors are apt to quote the multi-faceted account given by Harvey and Green (1993), working in the UK, who gave a range of concepts of quality in education such as:

- achieving excellence, the 'exceptional';
- 'perfection' (or consistency), such as demonstrating conformance to a standard;
- 'fitness-for-purpose ', appropriateness to situation;
- providing 'value-for-money'; and

the one that Harvey (1998) seems to prefer as being closest to the 'true nature' and purpose of the educational process:

- the 'transformation' (or improvement) of the learner, through the empowerment and value-adding effects of learning.

Thus, in many cases, as a researcher, one is using imperfect indicators to address a somewhat elusive construct.

This is even more pronounced when we look at issues such as 'employability'. Once again, we might imagine this to be a simple matter of looking at how readily employed graduates are – the proportion in employment six months after graduating, for example. Even with this kind of indicator, as Moreau and Leathwood (2006) point out, matters are complicated. Throughout the period that they studied, the graduate unemployment rate increased marginally, but as there were progressively more graduates pursuing work, the relative return for those having a degree decreased, too; especially for those holding degrees from the so-called new universities, those who were from working-class backgrounds and women. These groups tend to enjoy less of a 'graduate premium' than other groups. Therefore a construct like employability carries with it a number of other factors which it is not really in the power of the university to alter, no matter how much value it tries to add or how much it attempts to guide students into appropriate employment.

There are important factors at work constructing and creating the variables here. Rather than something that can readily be repackaged in terms of what Nussbaum called 'metricity', there are a variety of issues informing the construct which almost any possible measure will conflate and render the results confusing, no matter how numerically precise or reliable they may be. As Moreau and Leathwood (2006) describe, employability is often constructed as primarily a matter of an individual's skills. Hillage and Pollard state that:

> For the individual, employability depends on the knowledge, skills and aptitudes they possess, the way they use those assets and present them to employers and the context (e.g. personal circumstances and labour-market environment) within which they seek work. (Hillage and Pollard 1998: 2)

In the same vein, Yorke defines employability also in terms of a suite of individual features, making the construct difficult to measure or 'metricize'. It is:

> a set of achievements – skills, understandings and personal attributes – that make graduates more likely to gain employment and be successful in their chosen occupations, which benefits themselves, the workforce, the community and the economy. (Yorke 2004: 7)

As many have argued (Brown and Hesketh 2004, Moreau and Leathwood 2006), the use of the term 'employability' represents a shift of discourses. The terms used draw on different explanatory frameworks as to why a person might be employed or unemployed and different constructions of the worker. In discussing employment, there has been a 'shift from a systematic view of the labour market to a focus on the individuals and their qualities' (Garsten and Jacobsson 2003: 2). What might once have been called 'unemployment' is now more likely to be seen as an individual problem of 'employability'. The state has still retained an interest in the situation, but rather the focus is on how to equip individuals for a progressively more competitive 'knowledge-driven' economy and on 'empowering' them to take 'responsibility' for their own 'employability' so as to secure employment. Closely allied to this discourse of employability is the recent focus on 'skills', such that, in a climate of changing demands on the workforce, individuals are being made responsible for upgrading such 'perishable goods' through lifelong learning (Garsten and Jacobsson 2003, Moreau and Leathwood 2006). As suggested in the report 'Foundation Degrees: Meeting the need for higher level skills':

> If we want a competitive economy and an inclusive society we need more young people and adults to acquire higher level skills and knowledge. This is the era of lifelong learning with adults returning to learning full-time or part-time, often on more than one occasion in their lifetime in order to refresh their knowledge, upgrade their skills and sustain their employability. (DfES 2003: 5)

As Morley puts it:

> Arguably, employability is a decontextualised signifier in so far as it overlooks how structures such as gender, race, social class and disability interact with the labour market opportunities.
> (Morley 2001: 132)

From the point of view of doing research, this means that the question is one of whether we have added value to graduates in the course of their higher education. In addition, despite the best efforts of quality assurance people, degrees are not a uniform product, with wide differences in numbers of hours of study and degree classes obtained (Bekhradnia *et al.* 2006). Indeed, the relationship between the graduates' degrees and what has been added to their likely employment prospects is, in this latest formulation, part of a mysterious architecture inside their heads. So, knowing what we are doing if we seek to explore even an apparently simple question such as what we are adding to people by giving them opportunities to study in higher education is a complex one. Once we unpack what the variables mean and how different authors and policy-makers conceptualize them, it becomes much more difficult to research them meaningfully.

Realism: Variables, indicators and explanatory power

The problem of variables 'disappearing' when we subject them to scrutiny does not rule them out of scientific enquiry. The problem of their only being incompletely known, through rough approximations or indicators, is one which has been tackled through the brand of philosophy known as 'realism', or 'critical realism'. If you take a variable of interest, such as a graduate's 'employability' or their 'skills', you're not going to know these directly. You can build up an indirect picture through a variety of indicators, such as what they think they've gained themselves, how likely they are to be employed and what potential employers think of them. Likewise, if we are interested in stress among academic staff in the university system, this is a construct that we might tackle through indicators like people's responses on self-report questionnaires designed to measure occupational stress, absenteeism, turnover, reports of working hours and so on. The variables remain hypothetical constructs, but we can use these indicators to gain a sense of what they might be.

This situation has meant that the so-called 'realist' perspective has grown in popularity with many researchers. As an alternative to the position of positivism, the 'critical realist' or 'scientific realist' point of view retains a grip on the notion that there is an external reality 'out there' beyond our heads and notionally beyond the processes of enquiry we used to try to get at it. This perspective is associated with the work of Bhaskar who, from the 1970s to the present, has been leading development in the critical realist paradigm. This paradigm can be seen as a response to the problems of the positivist paradigm, but also it is a means of steering away from some of the approaches to social enquiry that make more tenuous claims about reality. Realists have sometimes been concerned about the way that more interpretive and postmodernist approaches have shied away from making any decisive statements about 'reality' at all. Social inequality makes a difference to a person's life chances; the likelihood of their attending university, the illnesses they will suffer from, the job they will be likely to do and how long they will live. A realist might well want to make some statement about these relationships while still acknowledging the difficulty of measuring these things. The critical realist would also want to make some statements about the nature of being or the 'ontology' concerning the phenomena they study. From a realist point of view something is *real* if it *can bring about visible or material consequences.* That is, in critical realism, something is taken to be *real* if it is *causally efficacious.* This includes things which the researcher finds difficult to see or experience directly, but which we have strong grounds for suspecting are causally effective, such as magnetic fields, 'unemployment' or 'poverty'. In terms of their position on whether 'the truth is out there' is indeed true, some critical realists adhere to a 'correspondence theory of truth' – suggesting that it is. Others opt for a more pragmatic account of truth – maybe reality is out there somewhere and all we can hope for is progressively more and more adaptive or practically fruitful approximations of it.

Another key difference between critical realism and much of the positivism that we discussed earlier concerns an issue known as methodological individualism. One of its proponents who takes it as his starting point is Jon Elster, who argues that:

> The elementary unit of social life is the individual human action. To explain social institutions and social change is to show how they arise as the result of the actions and interaction of individuals. This view, often referred to as methodological individualism, is in my view trivially true. (Elster 1989: 13)

Methodological individualism then involves this kind of reductionism. Mass social phenomena can be explained as resulting from the actions of the individuals who make them up – a position which as we saw earlier is associated with positivism. That is, it 'is the doctrine that facts about societies, and social phenomena generally are to be explained solely in terms of facts about individuals' (Bhaskar 1998: 27). Bhaskar also refers to what he calls *social atomism*, a similar form of explanation where social events are explained with reference to the behavior of the 'participating individuals' and the description of their situation.

Methodological individualism or social atomism are mistaken, according to Bhaskar, because 'explanation, whether by subsumption under general law, advertion to motives and rules, or redescription (identification), always involves irreducible social predicates' (Bhaskar 1998: 28). The individual actions, in other words, do not really explain anything because they only make sense in relation to larger wholes or social contexts. Filling in an application form for university presupposes that there's a university system to apply to. Adopting a particular kind of structured learning approach presupposes a particular kind of learning environment managed in a particular way. If one is a working-class student this presupposes that there is a working class to belong to, and so on.

In his book *The Possibility of Naturalism* (1998), Bhaskar argued that 'societies are irreducible to people'; that 'social forms are the necessary conditions for any internal act'; that the *pre-existence* of these social forms determines their *autonomy* as possible objects of scientific enquiry, and more importantly, that the *causal power* of these social forms determines their *reality* (Bhaskar 1998: 25).

On the one hand, Bhaskar (1998) argues that there can be such a thing as a *bona fide* science of individuals or of social phenomena, so in this sense naturalism is possible. That is, naturalism in the sense of a unity between the forms of enquiry, concepts and methods of the social and natural sciences. On the other hand, he does not want the kind of naturalism that collapses the social sciences entirely into the natural sciences or which reduces collective phenomena to the actions or decisions of individuals, brains or neurones.

One of the crucial aspects of Bhaskar's account of human enquiry from the point of view of social scientists engaged in research on the education system, is that he sees it as entirely legitimate to draw upon so-called transcendental arguments. A transcendental argument is one that starts with 'an agreed description of an event and then goes on to ask what mechanisms might exist for that event to be possible. The mechanisms in question might not be open to empirical observation but are nevertheless real and influential. Moreover, they can be subjected to critical, investigative enquiry' (Houston 2005: 9).

Thus, it is permissible to hypothesize that the construct of 'cultural capital' is important to success in the higher education system even though it is not a physical entity that we can see under a microscope, nor has it a monetary value. It is real because we can see its *effects*. 'The domain of the real is distinct from and greater than the domain of the empirical' (Bhaskar 1998: xii). Thus, if we can theorize about the presence and nature of these mechanisms and subsequently test their consequences, then we have the basis of a scientific method.

Looking for deep structure

Regarding the object of social science enquiry, Bhaskar argues that society is not created by human beings, yet is reproduced and transformed by them. In Bhaskar's *transformational model of social activity*, society and human activity have a *dual character*. 'Society is both the ever-present condition (material cause) and the continually reproduced outcome of human agency.' This is also called the *duality of structure*. 'And praxis is both work, that is, conscious *production*, and (normally unconscious) *reproduction* of the conditions of production, that is society.' This is what he terms the *duality of praxis* (Bhaskar 1998: 34–5). Human activity is characterized by intentionality, yet according to Bhaskar people, in their conscious activities, unconsciously *reproduce* and occasionally *transform* the structures governing their substantive activities of production (Bhaskar 1998: 35). As he puts it:

> People do not create society. For it always pre-exists them and is a necessary condition for their activity. Rather, society must be

> regarded as an ensemble of structures, practices and conventions which individuals reproduce or transform, but which would not exist unless they did so. Society does not exist independently of human activity (the error of reification). But it is not the product of it (the error of voluntarism). (Bhaskar 1998: 36)

As with the model of society and higher education proposed by the UK's DfES, in Bhaskar's view skills, competences and habits are acquired and maintained as necessary preconditions for reproducing and transforming society; this is the process of *socialization.* In Bhaskar's words:

> Society . . . provides necessary conditions for intentional human action, and intentional human action is a necessary condition for it. Society is only present in human action, but human action always expresses and utilizes some or other social form.
>
> (Bhaskar 1998: 34–5)

Thus, it is rather like Marx's famous dictum (quoted in Kamenka 1983: 287): 'Men [*sic*] make their own history, but not spontaneously, under conditions they have chosen for themselves; rather on terms immediately existing, given and handed to them.' The emphasis on human agency means that the 'actor's accounts form the indispensable starting point of social enquiry' (Bhaskar 1998: xvi). But unlike constructivist approaches, which accept all accounts as equally valid (Kenwood 1999), critical realism is open to the possibility of 'distorted perception'.

Sometimes the 'distorted perception' and 'false consciousness' can be relieved suddenly and painfully. Ball *et al.* (1999) discuss what they term 'learning identities' and describe how the structures of inequality intersect with the experiences students have as they go through the final years of school, undertake the UK's GCSEs at the age of 16 and then perhaps go on to undertake further training or study. Students and their families make educational career decisions in relative rather than absolute terms, according to their position in the social structure (Duru-Bellat 1996). Ball *et al.* see the experience of GCSE coursework and examinations as having a major impact on what they call young people's 'learning identities'. Sometimes, they say, the 'deep substructures of inequality' re-emerge clearly. Social class divisions, which up to that point had not been so conspicuous amongst the young people, suddenly became more important as the differentiation of routes and 'spaces' of opportunity began more forcefully to reproduce broader patterns of inequality. 'Privilege and disadvantage are ploughed into youth careers through family and education but most importantly at the interface between the two spheres' (Bates and Riseborough 1993: 9).

As Benton and Craib add, reinforcing the importance of attending to the deep structure of social reality:

> Modern science not only tells us of the existence of this unsuspected 'deep' structure in the world, but it also uses this to explain those aspects of the world which we do experience and acknowledge – such as the changes in the properties of foods when we cook them, the symptoms of illness we have, the similarities between parents and children and so on. Strict versions of empiricism have difficulty in accepting this as the core of scientific knowledge, since so many of these theoretical entities are not accessible to direct observation. (Benton and Craib 2001: 121)

Another way of making sense of this is through Bhaskar's distinction between the 'transitive' or epistemological dimension of reality from its 'intransitive' dimension. The transitive dimension comprises our perception of reality, whilst the intransitive dimension is the actual – the 'real', the 'material' – underlying structure of reality.

In Bhaskar's view, one of the key purposes in engaging in social science research in the first place is so that we can make the world a better place. His vision is, like Marxism, programmatic. Bhaskar asked: 'What is the relationship between the relational conception of sociology and the transformational model of social activity?' His answer was that human agency must be linked to social structures by an enduring *point of contact* that is occupied by individuals. This mediating system is what Bhaskar called the position–practice system (Bhaskar 1998: 40–41). An important theme in his work is the need to expose and lessen the unpleasant effects of the mechanisms which promote oppression and suffering. There is a moral imperative in social science: Bhaskar contends that if researchers discover suffering or disadvantage through our enquiry, then we must consider and implement ways of reducing that suffering. If we find 'false consciousness' which disadvantages people then we are equipped to do something about it:

> If one is in possession of a theory that explains why false consciousness is necessary, then one can pass immediately, without the addition of any extraneous value judgement, to a negative evaluation on the object that makes such consciousness necessary and to a positive evaluation on action rationally directed at removing it.
>
> (Bhaskar 1991: 473)

As Houston (2001) explains, this emancipatory thrust to Bhaskar's work is facilitated through the process of *retroduction*. This process is proposed as an alternative to induction (where perceptions are generated from experience) and deduction (where perceptions are developed from axioms and logical thought). Instead, it is concerned with constructing plausible models that provisionally explain how certain events unfold. In undertaking retroduction the investigator attempts to identify patterns of behaviour that appear to highlight underlying structures, constructs or processes. A number of *a priori* hypotheses about the mechanisms giving rise to these phenomena can then be formulated. To get the best out of them, these hypotheses are framed using relevant explanatory theories that have a demonstrable value in identifying causal factors. It is valuable to use theories that have already shown their explanatory power in similar situations so that novel phenomena can be linked with things that are already known. The next stage in retroduction involves testing the hypotheses. To what extent do they provide adequate explanations of the phenomena under scrutiny? The researcher then tries to find supportive – and also disconfirming – evidence (Popper 1959) to challenge the hypotheses against the available data. Finally, once our hypotheses have withstood our attempts to disconfirm them and they appear to have some validity, then we are at the 'point of contact' mentioned earlier and we can intervene strategically and purposefully to ameliorate any deleterious effects of the mechanisms we have identified.

The process of identifying the causal laws or deep structures which propel the events one observes is always a difficult one. While patterns of events can readily be observed, there are relatively few circumstances under which these laws can be identified. Bhaskar makes a sharp distinction between 'patterns of events' and 'causal laws'. Like many philosophers of science, he grants a special place to experiments in this process:

> What is so special about the patterns [that scientists] deliberately produce under meticulously controlled conditions in the laboratory is that it enables them to identify the mode of operation of natural structures, mechanisms or processes which they do not produce. What distinguishes the phenomena the scientist *actually* produces from the totality of the phenomena she *could* produce is that, when her experiment is successful, it is an index of what she does *not* produce. A *real* distinction between the objects of experimental investigation, such as causal laws, and patterns of events, is thus a condition of the intelligibility of experimental activity.
>
> (Bhaskar 1998: 9, emphasis in original)

The causal laws of nature therefore are invisible, yet embedded in the natural structure under investigation. They are therefore different from the empirical patterns of events. To fully understand the event in question, we must be alert to this distinction. This ontological distinction applies for social as well as natural phenomena.

This also highlights one of the parallels Bhaskar detects between the social and natural sciences: from the point of view of his critical naturalism, the structure of generation of knowledge is comparable in both natural and social science. Thus, there is a 'methodological unity' in the practice of science that cuts across many fields of human enquiry.

In conclusion: Positivism, realism and critical educational enquiry

Finally, let us return from this excursion into Bhaskar's account of scientific enquiry and ask what parallels we can find between this and the study of educational processes. So far, our exposition has involved chunks of theory from the philosophy of science without much leavening of detailed, worked through, examples of educational research.

In part, this is because the practical business of research often takes a good deal for granted. Research reports seldom dig at the roots of their own research methodology and epistemology. Researchers often assume that the constructs they are looking for are there somewhere under the forest of clues and indicators that they have to sift through. In researching widening access to higher education, for example, one might assume that the constructs of 'social class', 'disadvantage' and 'barriers' to access are there somewhere under the data about family income levels, first-person accounts from students, and government statistics about participation rates. There is an act of imagination in seeking the links and detecting the constructs, like seeing the fish in a murky pond. This is something that researchers are often rather coy about, lest it disturb the mantle of scientism and rigour which they have so carefully drawn around themselves.

Another reason why the field of education studies is not yet replete with references to Bhaskar is that they have their own theoretical champion in the form of Pierre Bourdieu, who is increasingly recognized as having a good deal in common with realism as propounded by Bhaskar himself (Nash 2003).

Both Bourdieu and Bhaskar would acknowledge that developing appropriate methods for exploring and synthesizing knowledge of very different sets of human needs and interests from different socials groups is no easy thing to do. From Bourdieu's point of view, those groups whose cultural capital is not valued by high-status interests in society will very likely be misunderstood by social scientists. A group lacking in high status or in highly valued cultural capital, such as those who are excluded from the education system, would probably provide very different accounts of their own intentions and behaviour than those provided for them by a dominant group. They may seem difficult as a result, or even obtuse, perverse or wrong. Consequently, these accounts are discounted or stigmatized. For Bourdieu, much social analysis of practical questions misses the unique features of people's understanding and action in a situation and instead applies a normalizing formula which renders the situation understandable to academics, but further distances the researcher from the people and the social field that is under scrutiny. Like Bhaskar, Bourdieu acknowledges that there are many possible sets of ethnic, gender and class interests that are very different from one another and do require different and perhaps incompatible strategies of enquiry, which might not be appreciated by anyone who is not steeped in the relevant class, gender or minority culture:

> realists attempt to take on board some of the insights of hermeneutics and Wittgenstein. Like Shutz and Winch, they see the social world as pregnant with meaning. Against structuralist or functionalist sociology, they tend to emphasize that people are not 'cultural dopes'. People are considered to be knowledgeable, and that knowledgeability tends to be practical and embedded in the taken-for-granted nature of everyday activities. (Baert 1996: 516)

Thus, after our tour through two kinds of philosophy of science that are based on the claim that 'the truth is out there', we can see how this apparently commonsensical assertion has yielded so much uncertainty. The positivists, despite their determination to avoid religion and metaphysics and to base their accounts of phenomena entirely upon observation, found themselves experiencing increasing doubt as to what it was they were observing. In a sense, the direction in which positivism was propelled by Otto Neurath was more radically sceptical of truth claims than any later postmodernist. Despite the radical, revolutionary and emancipatory fervour that gripped positivism from the mid-nineteenth century to the 1940s and despite the strong feminist sentiments expressed by Comte, it has subsequently become a byword for research which is mindlessly empiricist and which appears to uphold the interests of dominant groups.

The realist perspective, as we have seen, has recently been proposed as a replacement philosophy for the present generation of socially engaged, politically savvy social scientists who believe that there is a material reality that structures people's experiences and life chances but are appropriately sceptical of how readily we can measure it. Despite this uncertainty, people are fairly sure it's out there somewhere. It allows them to rely upon factors and variables which are hypothetical constructs and cannot be directly observed but which are believed to have explanatory power. Lest this be thought a rather unscientific thing to do, it can be pointed out that this reasoning strategy can be observed on the part of many 'hard' scientists, whose laboratory instruments can give only indicative evidence of underlying entities and processes. Realism also provides the kind of framework into which many different kinds of human enquiry can be arranged. The process of testing hypotheses, for example, can be seen as one special part of a whole suite of activities that occur in the process of human enquiry.

The question of reality and whether it is something we can approach knowledge of in our research remains, however, a vexed one, as we shall see in the next chapter. Research that adds to our theoretical sophistication may nevertheless contain a curious gap between theory and findings. Sometimes the inferences made from the data to hand are used to support accounts of society so grand that one can virtually hear them creaking under the weight. Appeals to reality or materiality then, seldom lead to certainty. More usually, they open up further areas for discussion and disagreement.

3

Interpretative approaches, ethnographies of higher education and the description of experience

Introduction: Different research traditions

This chapter represents a shift of gear from the previous one. Here we shall be discussing attempts to interpret the social and experiential world found in education and in particular in universities. This has recently been the subject of some interest due to changes that have taken place in higher education in the last few years. First, there is increasing interest in the learning processes which education encourages, particularly in the light of the perceived need to train staff in teaching, to assess quality and to enable a wider variety of participants than were previously included to enjoy a university education. This has necessitated a good deal of attention to the learner's experience, such that their impressions of university or college have been probed, as well as their experience of learning and the intersection of the university experience with factors such as the learner's life histories, financial situation and childcare responsibilities. On the face of it, this kind of investigation might sound straightforward and a great deal should be possible merely by talking to people and keeping one's eyes and ears open.

However, as the reader might suspect by now, this is not quite so simple. Different research styles tend to bring with them different kinds of assumptions. To explore the implications of this a little more fully let us draw a few lessons from the history and philosophy of science. A good deal of the twentieth century's philosophy of science has been dominated by the revolutionary changes in physics in the late nineteenth century and early twentieth century, as the discipline moved from classical mechanics through to new theories of relativity and quantum mechanics. There appeared to be a sudden change in the way scholars thought about the processes of enquiry and identified significant problems to be solved.

The paradigm shifts: Kuhn and the structure of scientific revolutions

Around the middle of the twentieth century, this process of sudden changes in scientific disciplines fascinated a graduate student of physics at Harvard University by the name of Kuhn (1922–96). Later, through the 1950s and 1960s, he found his way into teaching the history of science, and eventually published his observations in 1962 as *The Structure of Scientific Revolutions* which rapidly gained him a place as one of the best-known and most-cited figures in the philosophy of science.

Kuhn was most famous for what he said about paradigms. Indeed, he was the person who took the word away from its previous, highly specific use in linguistics and gave it more general currency as a way of describing a model, a mindset and a way of knowing. In particular, he used it to refer to a set of practices that define a scientific discipline during a particular period of time. Kuhn defined a paradigm as: 'an entire constellation of beliefs, values and techniques, and so on, shared by the members of a given community' (Kuhn 1970: 175).

In his later work, Kuhn himself came to prefer other terms such as 'exemplar' and 'normal science' to characterize the mindset and models used by particular scientific communities. However, in *The Structure of Scientific Revolutions*, Kuhn identifies the following features of scientific paradigms. They determine:

- *what* is to be observed and scrutinized
- the kind of *questions* that are supposed to be asked and probed for answers in relation to this subject
- *how* these questions are to be structured
- *how* the results of scientific investigations should be interpreted.

Thus, when scientists in a particular discipline share a paradigm then the advance of knowledge looks remarkably sprightly: 'one of the things a scientific community acquires with a paradigm is a criterion for choosing problems that, while the paradigm is taken for granted, can be assumed to have solutions' (Kuhn 1970: 37). 'One of the reasons why normal science seems to progress so rapidly is that its practitioners concentrate on problems that only their own lack of ingenuity should keep them from solving' (Kuhn 1970:37). The paradigm then enables them to all play the game to the same rules. This then is what Kuhn called 'normal science', where everyone in the scientific community proceeds with the solution of a common set of problems with a common set of methods.

Over time, there are an increasing number of findings that do not fit and a growing awareness of areas of nature that the prevailing paradigm cannot address. Under such circumstances, there may be a relatively rapid change in the paradigm which a research community uses. 'Successive transition from one paradigm to another via revolution is the usual developmental pattern of mature science' (Kuhn 1970: 12). The question of whether a paradigm will be changed is not always entirely a rational one. The 'issue of paradigm choice is not settled by logic and experiment alone'. New paradigms make different predictions and attend to different phenomena. In this way, knowledge expands its reach 'to areas and to degrees of precision for which there is no full precedent' (Kuhn 1970: 100).

Kuhn's idea was itself revolutionary, as it initiated some far-reaching changes in the way that people talked about scientific enquiry and scientific change. Thus, it was itself part of its own 'paradigm shift' in the history and sociology of science.

This idea of paradigms changing, which was originally part of the effort on the part of philosophers of science to come to terms with changes in physics around a century ago, has proved especially popular in the social sciences where it has become a means of describing the sheer variety of schools of thought and practices of enquiry. Here, there is seldom revolutionary change in the way that Kuhn envisaged. Researchers do not all suddenly switch from one paradigm to another. Rather, there is a good deal of coexistence and parallel development, as well as the occasional moment of friction and conflict.

To add to the development of the paradigm concept, a number of authors have applied it to different domains. Kilbourne (2006) describes how cultures themselves can embody dominant social paradigms. Milbrath (1984: 7) defines a culture's dominant social paradigm as comprising 'the values, metaphysical beliefs, institutions, habits, etc., that collectively provide social lenses through which individuals and groups interpret their social world'. In Cotgrove's (1982) formulation, the dominant social paradigm is not necessarily just the one to which the majority of people adhere. Rather, it is the one held by dominant groups in society. In this way, it helps to legitimatize and justify the prevailing activities and institutions that promote the interests of those dominant groups. In doing this, it also serves as a justification for social and political action. The key feature of a dominant social paradigm, according to Kilbourne (2006) is that it is 'introjected within society'. This means that its stipulations and justifications are readily accepted as truth, and do not require any further examination (Kilbourne 1998). A dominant social paradigm can have many dimensions, including political, economic and technological aspects within its structure.

New paradigms: Interpretative methods in the social and educational sciences

There is a good deal of research in the social sciences which seeks to make sense of the social world through a process of interpretation, which might involve texts, naturally occurring conversations, interviews and even descriptions of patterns of behaviour. Qualitative research materials may also include video and audio recordings, performances, celebrations, ceremonies, computer games, newspapers, government policy documents, cartoons and virtually everything else from which that social life is made. There are a bewildering variety of methods which seek to explore this cornucopia of materials, too. Old staples like ethnography and grounded theory jostle for space with relative newcomers, such as interpretative phenomenological analysis. We will not be cataloguing all the different kinds of research in the qualitative paradigm. First, there are many books that do this far more comprehensively than we have space for (Denzin *et al.* 2005, Marshall and Rossman 2006). Second, any such catalogue is bound to date quite quickly as new varieties of enquiry are developed. There is a bewildering proliferation of types and styles of contemporary qualitative research: the postmodern turn, the post-structuralist turn, the narrative turn (Denzin *et al.* 2006), and in progressive qualitative research in education there has been a turn to cultural studies (Dolby and Dimitriadis 2004, Wright 2006).

In investigating educational phenomena, there are many tempting reasons to select qualitative methodologies, yet many people still remain unfamiliar with the methods. There is still a divide within the social sciences, in that researchers trained in the use of quantitative designs have some difficulty when the need arises to use or teach qualitative research (Stallings 1995). There is, however, a growing body of literature devoted to qualitative research in education. For some time, researchers have debated the relative value of qualitative and quantitative paradigms of enquiry (Patton 1990). Much qualitative enquiry uses a naturalistic approach and seeks to understand phenomena in context-specific settings. This contrasts with much quantitative research, which attempts where possible to use experimental methods and quantitative measures to test pre-formulated hypotheses. Thus, the two traditions of research represent fundamentally different paradigms of enquiry, and research activity is based on the underlying assumptions of each paradigm.

In very broad brush strokes, qualitative research means 'any kind of research that produces findings not arrived at by means of statistical procedures or other means of quantification' (Strauss and Corbin 1990: 17). While quantitative research is often geared towards the identification of causes and the ability to predict, through the acquisition of generalizable findings; qualitative researchers instead seek to illuminate, understand and deduce findings that can be extrapolated to similar situations. Qualitative analysis, therefore, yields a different type of knowledge than that from quantitative enquiry, with the implication that it should be used in different ways.

There are, however, some parallels between qualitative and quantitative enquiry. Eisner (1991) argues that all our knowledge, whether it has been gained through qualitative or quantitative research, is referenced in qualities, and that our understanding of the world can be represented in many possible ways:

> There is a kind of continuum that moves from the fictional that is 'true' – the novel, for example – to the highly controlled and quantitatively described scientific experiment. Work at either end of this continuum has the capacity to inform significantly. Qualitative research and evaluation are located toward the fictive end of the continuum without being fictional in the narrow sense of the term.
> (Eisner 1991: 30–1)

Even those who have made their careers out of quantitative research are sometimes profoundly sensitive to what all the human activity under scrutiny means. Veteran educational researcher Lee J. Cronbach (1975: 126) argued that 'the special task of the social scientist in each generation is to pin down the contemporary facts. Beyond that, he shares with the humanistic scholar and the artist in the effort to gain insight into contemporary relationships.' Cronbach's experience over many years of statistical research led him to the claim that this mode of enquiry cannot take full account of the many interaction effects that occur in social settings. There are many examples of empirical 'laws' that do not hold true in actual settings, so Cronbach (1975: 124) states that 'the time has come to exorcise the null hypothesis' because it ignores effects that may be important, but which cannot achieve statistical significance. Qualitative enquiry accepts the complex and dynamic quality of the social world.

Paradigm wars?

Despite these kinds of conciliatory movements, the relationship between qualitative and quantitative research in educational enquiry has not always been an easy one. Wright (2006) characterizes the period from 1970 to 1986 as a 'paradigm war'. There was, says Wright, a momentous confrontation between quantitative and qualitative research in education. Quantitative research had been virtually synonymous with educational research until the 1970s, and with this era came a growing interest amongst educational researchers in qualitative research and a corresponding shift towards issues best addressed by qualitative research (McDiarmid 1976), which provoked a somewhat tense paradigmatic debate. This debate was chronicled in the US in a number of writings (e.g. Smith 1983, Smith and Heshusius 1986, Howe 1988) in the journal *Educational Researcher*.

However, it is not always necessary to pit the qualitative and quantitative paradigms against one another in a competing stance. By the 1990s, a different stance had emerged, Patton (1990: 39) advocated a 'paradigm of choices' that sought '*methodological appropriateness* as the primary criterion for judging methodological quality'. This would enable a 'situational responsiveness' that strict adherence to a single paradigm would not achieve. Furthermore, a growing number of researchers came to believe that qualitative and quantitative research can be effectively combined in the same research project (Patton 1990, Strauss and Corbin 1990).

Strauss and Corbin (1990) claim that qualitative methods can be used to increase our understanding of any social or educational phenomenon about which we know little. Qualitative methodology can also be used to develop new perspectives on things about which we already know a great deal, but about which we are seeking to gain new insights or generate new hypotheses. We may wish to gain more in-depth information that may be difficult to acquire in a quantitative manner. Thus, qualitative methods are often used in contexts where there is a desire to identify the variables that might later be examined, or generate hypotheses that may be tested quantitatively, or where it is believed that quantitative measures cannot entirely grasp a situation. In much qualitative enquiry, research problems tend to be framed as open-ended questions that will support the discovery of new information.

Novelties and complexities: The strengths of interpretive research

The possibility of qualitative research illustrating something new about an issue that we already know, is illustrated in a paper by Reay (2005), who describes the progress through school and to university of a number of young people in London. They came from a variety of different class positions and, in many cases, they had a strong sense of their place in a kind of social pecking order and what difference this made to their opportunities. Now, as we know, the UK government has been keen to encourage more youngsters into higher education and, at present, this seems to have enjoyed less success than policy-makers would like. Even though in the space of a single article there is room for only a few examples, we can gain some insight into why this process is difficult for many young people, especially those from the kinds of backgrounds the government is concerned with increasing participation. From the point of view of someone from a working-class or ethnic-minority background, attending university often involves the choice to both move away and become different to the natal family. In Reay's participants, it sometimes evoked 'powerful feelings of anxiety, loss, guilt and fear alongside the more accepted emotional responses of hopeful anticipation, excitement and pride' (Reay 2005: 921). This 'emotional tightrope' was especially apparent in the narratives of working-class students applying to go to university (Reay *et al.* 2005):

> Yes, it's been really really difficult. It ended up being really stressful because I was doing it in such a void. It's been really scary thinking that you could have made the wrong decision, very anxiety inducing . . . I think it's more difficult if no one in your family's been there. I think in a funny sort of way it's more difficult if you're black too . . . Because you want to go to a good university but you don't want to stick out like a sore thumb. It's a bit sad isn't it. I've sort of avoided all the universities with lots of black students because they're all the universities which aren't seen as so good. If you're black and not very middle class and want to do well then you end

up choosing places where people like you don't go and I think that's difficult.

(Candice, black working-class student, predicted two As and a B at A level) (Reay 2005: 921)

This narrative reveals a great deal about the process of choosing to go to university that is missing from official accounts. Here is a young black woman who is, in choosing to attend an elite university, cutting herself adrift from her moorings. It is also a matter of doing so in a 'void' because there is no family stock of wisdom on the matter and therefore considerable uncertainty as to whether the 'right' choice has been made.

As Hoepfl (1997) notes in her efforts to promote qualitative research in the discipline of technology and design education, qualitative enquiry's ability to more fully describe phenomena is important. 'If you want people to understand better than they otherwise might, provide them information in the form in which they usually experience it' (Lincoln and Guba 1985: 120). Qualitative research reports, with their ability to be enriched with detail and insights into participants' experiences of the world, 'may be epistemologically in harmony with the reader's experience' (Stake 1978: 5) and thus may be more meaningful.

Hoepfl (1997) provides a synthesis of several writers' accounts of what they consider to be the prominent characteristics of qualitative, or naturalistic, research (e.g. Bogdan and Biklen 1982, Lincoln and Guba 1985, Patton 1990, Eisner 1991). Hoepfl summarizes their characterizations of qualitative research as follows (Hoepfl 1997: 49):

1) Qualitative research uses the natural setting as the source of data. The researcher attempts to observe, describe and interpret settings as they are, maintaining what Patton (1990: 55) calls an 'empathic neutrality'.
2) The researcher acts as the 'human instrument' of data collection.
3) Qualitative researchers predominantly use inductive data analysis.

4) Qualitative research reports are descriptive, incorporating expressive language and the 'presence of voice in the text' (Eisner 1991: 36).
5) Qualitative research has an interpretive character, aimed at discovering the meaning events have for the individuals who experience them, and the interpretations of those meanings by the researcher.
6) Qualitative researchers pay attention to the idiosyncratic as well as the pervasive, seeking the uniqueness of each case.
7) Qualitative research has an emergent (as opposed to predetermined) design, and researchers focus on this emerging process as well as the outcomes or product of the research.
8) Qualitative research is judged using particular criteria for trustworthiness according to Lincoln and Guba (1985: 290): 'How can an inquirer persuade his or her audiences that the research findings of an inquiry are worth paying attention to?'

These are not 'absolute characteristics of qualitative enquiry, but rather strategic ideals that provide a direction and a framework for developing specific designs and concrete data collection tactics' (Hoepfl 1997: 51, Patton 1990: 59). These characteristics are considered to be 'interconnected' (Patton 1990: 40) and 'mutually reinforcing' (Lincoln and Guba 1985: 39). Often a qualitative research design is an 'emergent' one. Because the researcher seeks to observe and interpret meanings in context, it is neither possible nor appropriate to finalize research strategies before data collection has begun (Hoepfl 1997, Patton 1990). The design of qualitative studies depends on the purpose of the inquiries and will involve consideration of what information will be most useful, and what data will have the most credibility. There are often no formal criteria for determining sample size (Patton 1990). 'Qualitative studies typically employ multiple forms of evidence. . . . [and] there is no statistical test of significance to determine if results "count"' (Eisner 1991: 39). Judgements about usefulness and credibility are left to the researcher and the reader to make, often in the light of the kinds of ethical or political commitments the researchers have.

Value commitments in qualitative research

In Chapter 2 we mentioned the way that a political or moral imperative is involved in research from a critical realist perspective. In the same way, researchers involved in qualitative enquiry often align themselves with particular political imperatives, perhaps intended to challenge inequalities or promote wider access to educational experiences of the kind that have traditionally been restricted to elites.

Thus, as Hammersley (1995) identifies, judgements by researchers are frequently made about the moral or political character of those being studied to maintain the researcher's position and we literally arrive at a situation involving 'goodies and baddies'. This was evident when the authors reviewed a body of widening participation research (Baker *et al.* 2006) and found that in much of this research, the perceptions of students' perceptions were granted a particular privilege in the research. This might appear laudable given that they represent a group whose views might be important to the debate about widening participation in higher education. However, this point of view was used to paint a consistently negative picture of the comments and actions of academic staff, sometimes to the point of demonizing them. In much of this research, academic staff were identified as the 'problem', and complicit agents in the structure responsible for the oppression. This goes beyond taking what participants say seriously and treats what they say in an unmediated fashion as if it were a veridical analysis of the university system.

Whereas it is important not to minimize the difficulties of being a student, for a variety of humanitarian reasons, much of the literature on widening access to higher education involves actively sustaining some curious blind spots. For example, it is well documented that academic staff themselves have lost a great deal of their autonomy, status and power in recent years (Furedi 2004, Evans 2005, Baker and Brown 2007), yet this is strangely absent from much of the widening access literature which under-theorizes the constraints imposed on higher education institutions by societal factors and government policies. For example, Bowl (2000: 34) quotes one of her interviewees regarding financial worries:

> I don't think they're helpful at all really [. . .] There's no backup, no support [. . .] And when I talked to my tutor about my grant thing, he said: 'Oh well you'd better get that cleared up, because [the HEI] don't hang about waiting for people to pay their tuition fees. They're going to come after you'. (Bowl 2000: 34)

This was used as an example of an unhelpful tutor. Yet read in another way, this could be a tutor sympathizing with a student over a draconian regime. With any knowledge of how higher education institutions work, it would be clear that the tutor quoted would be most unlikely to be able to intervene in this situation in the way that the student – or Bowl herself – would hope.

Likewise, the expectations of academic work in a university context are given short shrift in the widening access literature. Bamber and Tett (2001) are extensively critical of these academic expectations:

> The students report that engaging with literature, having to produce formal essays and comply with all the other aspects of academic literacies, often seems like unnecessary hoop-jumping. Some retain a distrust of academic language and struggle to master it throughout the length of the course.
>
> (Bamber and Tett 2001: 12)

Bamber *et al.* also suggest that 'texts that are inaccessible to all but the most academically able could set back, rather than enhance, intellectual development' (2001: 14). Their extensive critique of the day-to-day expectations of academia suggests that the authors of this literature are expecting higher education to fulfil a role radically different from that which has traditionally been expected of it. It is as if these requirements, rather than being part of a particular scholarly tradition, are imposed frivolously and awkwardly by the staff themselves, which again under-theorizes how academic disciplines and academic practice have come to look the way they do.

This is the kind of manoeuvre that Hammersley (1995: 43–4) describes when talking about critical research, such that 'political goals override commitment to the production of knowledge'. There is also pressure from researchers themselves to define their goal in practical or political terms. These constraints are especially true in research committed to emancipatory politics, such as widening participation research. Thus, the goal of enquiry has been redefined as the promotion of some practical or political cause. Hammersely believes this must be resisted – such ideas threaten to destroy the proper operation of social research communities. Yet there is no defence in the absence of a convincing, post-foundationalist understanding of the nature of 'error' and 'bias' in social enquiry.

There is a powerful drift of opinion among researchers committed to interpretative approaches to the effect that all knowledge must be treated as serving the interests of those who produce or sponsor it. This view is very influential among widening access researchers. This tends to yield a simplistic and polarized account of the tensions, forces or powers which may be identifiable in any research situation. Certainly, a strong case can be made to the effect that knowledge does reflect the interests of powerful groups in society, but in practice this is often reduced to a simple formula to the effect that this is *all* knowledge ever does. This under-theorizes the nature of knowledge itself by a considerable margin. It also under-specifies the nature of institutions and organizations and how they arrive at their policies, customs and practices.

For example, as we have discussed elsewhere (Baker *et al.* 2006) there is a groundswell of opinion to the effect that the present UK higher education system tends to value only 'middle-class' knowledge, with the implication that the academy must adjust to other styles of life and forms of knowledge if it is to appropriately welcome non-traditional students. For example, Thomas (2002: 440) urges that the virtues of an inclusive learning experience are maximized if students are 'not expected to change to fit in with institutional expectations which are very different to there (*sic*) own'.

As Hammersley (1995) notes, this kind of thinking leads to the call for social research to be explicitly reorientated towards emancipatory political goals, and even to be openly partisan or ideological. In this spirit, many widening access researchers take this stance, perhaps most clearly articulated by Marion Bowl who explicitly identifies herself as working within a 'social justice framework' which involves her 'taking sides' (Bowl 2000: 33), that in practice means taking the students' side and foregrounding their grievances, as if these constituted an analysis in themselves.

Carspecken and Apple (1992: 512) say that 'the critical approach to field research is distinguished first of all in terms of the motivation of the researcher and the questions that are posed. Critical researchers are usually politically minded people who wish, through their research, to aid struggles against inequality and domination.' Researchers such as Marion Bowl and Liz Thomas are clearly in this category. As Hammersley says, 'here, we have reduction of concept of critique found in critical theory, to political criticism of society' (Hammersley 1995: 518). Sheer commitment to values matters, rather than rational justification. In some of the work we have just described, it is as if the very possibility of knowledge is undermined and is subsumed to the imperative to get more students into higher education. Understanding why institutions look the way they do and why academic knowledge looks like it does is obviated in the light of the injustice of students having to change their *habitus*, or the way they read, write and think. Because opinion is substituted for sociologically rigorous analysis of the situation, the position occupied by socially committed research undermines itself because it then becomes impossible to justify one's own particular political judgement and ideals against others (Dews 1987). Ethnographic researchers used to talk of the problems involved in 'going native' and absorbing so much of the culture, attitudes and worldview of the people being studied that one cannot do analysis upon it.

This illustrates the tightrope walked by researchers seeking to interpret the social world. On the one hand, there is often a strong temptation to right the perceived injustices and be socially committed, as in the realist approach outlined in the previous chapter. On the other hand, there is the tension Hammersley identifies between doing research that attempts to retain a fidelity to the research situation and the imperative of one's political or moral commitments as a researcher.

This is not to suggest that 'objectivity' is possible in any simple sense, since when one strips away the veneer of respectability attached to the term, it is usual to find the partiality of a dominant group at work. However, there are difficulties of which the novice researcher and the informed reader of research reports should be aware.

Making things more complex

A feature of the social world that qualitative research highlights is that things are often more complicated than they seem. The blocks of people who appear in statistics and in much quantitative research are much more differentiated in their views, opinions, interests, and in terms of their ways of navigating through the world, than might at first appear. That is, the categories like 'working class', 'women' and 'ethnic minority' sometimes seem at odds with people's narrative accounts of what they are doing. Like the black student in Diane Reay's research mentioned above, people's engagement with these emblockments is often partial and ambivalent and they are sometimes not a coherent group with a common set of interests.

Consider the position of women as workers within universities. As Morley (1999) points out, there is often an assumption in much of the literature on women's working lives that being female means that a woman will be accommodating, collegial and supportive to other women. However, in several papers by Skelton (2004, 2005a, 2005b) there were many instances of women feeling particularly badly treated by other women in their university careers. Here are a couple of examples of what Skelton's participants said. The names of people about whom they were speaking have been substituted by square brackets.

> Elizabeth: [Feminist academic] was an amazingly important person in my academic career . . . she was very generous to me but I could never understand myself in relation to her as owning any of the work. . . . I was so shadowed by her . . . it was very difficult and the

> questions of ownership became the site of such struggle between us. She didn't really encourage the people she worked with to write independently of her.
>
> Angela: Although we've got [name] who saw herself as a feminist . . . her practice is the opposite, quite diabolical in the way she operates . . . she will not have strong women anywhere near her. . . . What's so galling is [women] who presented themselves in the past as a feminist. [Name] is a classic Thatcherite in that sense, pulling the ladder up after her. (Skelton 2005a: 328)

Thus, the opportunity exists in qualitative research to unpack some of the broader sociological categories to reveal friction and turbulence within them and to problematize aggregated demographic categories and ideas we might entertain about common interest groups. In the same way, an outsider's vision of 'the community' as an integrated whole may mask frictions, tensions and divisions which are more apparent to those who are intimately involved.

Nevertheless, there is sometimes a tendency among researchers and among important gatekeepers such as editors to expect the social world to turn out to be a certain way. Patterns of inequality, occupations and oppressions are seen in a particular way and exceptions to the expected pattern often involve an uphill struggle in order to gain credence. In other words, the 'paradigm' as Kuhn would describe it, is working to control the kinds of things that can be said within the framework of social enquiry. Knowledge, in a sense, is about what one leaves out as well as what one puts in. Hammersley and Gomm (2000) note that in some research traditions an 'epistemic paradigm' is enforced such that scope for internal dissent is restricted.

We have encountered some interesting examples of this when our own work has been reviewed. We were recently involved in life-narrative work of people who grew up in rural Welsh-language communities during the latter half of the last century, and were particularly interested in participants who had experienced severe socio-economic disadvantage. Some of the reviewers' comments on parts of this work illustrate the mechanisms through which fidelity to the dominant paradigm is enforced. A number of our participants were the children of hill farmers in the Snowdonia area of Wales. Anyone familiar with the history and geography of the region will be aware that many hill-farming families endured (and continue to endure) severe hardship. Their level of education was usually low, their incomes were frequently very limited and the amount of work involved in their lifestyle was substantial. We know people from this cohort who endured disadvantages as severe as any other group whose hardship may be more familiar to people outside of rural Wales. In presenting this material for publication, this hardship was identified, and we alluded to this region having a culture somewhat different to many other parts of the UK. Yet one reviewer maintained that these people could not be considered disadvantaged 'because they are farmers and farmers are middle class', and another reviewer maintained that the distinction between 'farmers' or 'tenant farmers' would be crucial in determining the level of disadvantage experienced, displaying some ignorance of patterns of land use, tenancy and proprietorship in the area concerned. Thus to those twenty-first-century researchers who are more familiar with the urban, English disadvantaged, and with a picture of farming drawn from the more extensively subsidised agriculture of the south of England, the hardship experienced by our participants was readily dismissed. It is processes like this which ensure that the disadvantage we read about in periodicals concerned with sociology or education is overwhelmingly urban, and that participants are not allowed certain job titles and, if in an ethnolinguistic minority, they need to be in one that is 'acceptable', rather than, for example, Welsh. Our participants and their life stories fell outside of the epistemic paradigm.

This mirrors the way in which many indigenous people have undertaken considerable struggles to have their voices heard in a social science environment which privileges particular ways of doing things and ways of seeing the world. As Denzin *et al.* (2006) have noted, the past few years have seen many indigenous scholars attempting to get the academy to 'decolonize' its scientific practices (Grande 2004, Battiste 2006, Smith 2006). At the same time, these scholars have sought to disrupt traditional ways of knowing, while developing 'methodologies and approaches to research that privileged indigenous knowledges, voices and experiences' (Smith 2005: 87). In the face of this, positivist researchers often retreat into a value-free objectivist science model to defend their position. They seldom attempt to make explicit – let alone critique – the 'moral and political commitments in their own contingent work' (Carey 1989: 104).

Perhaps an even more obvious example of the moral and political commitments of the adherents of a particular epistemic paradigm leading them to invalidate participants' accounts was shown by a reviewer's comment on a quote from a participant of ours who said, when comparing her life after arriving at university with that before:

> I never particularly expected to even do A levels let alone go to university, so my life is very much divided into before and after . . . before university my morals were very much that you grew up, had five different children by different rubbish men who then went off and left you on the dole with the kids and that's pretty much what I thought my grown-up life would be . . . [university was] massively life changing, just from the very first moment I got there . . . things like having a wonderful grand meal in a hall full of three different sets of cutlery . . . it was like being in a film straight away and since then my life just completely changed . . . it's just really changed what I can do, who I can be, all aspects of my life.

This participant had endured a particularly difficult, disadvantaged upbringing and talked extensively of the epiphany that university life had been. Yet a reviewer commented that she 'had a pathological view of her own background'. Not only is this a highly invalidating comment made in the face of a dissenting view, but also displays a high level of paternalism being shown by someone who would otherwise subscribe to a radical, emancipatory stance. This is reminiscent of the kind of enquiry – undertaken for example from Marxist, feminist or critical realist points of view – where researchers come to believe that participants possess what

Engels called a 'false consciousness', who do not realize that they are victims of an unequal society and are 'deceived' into believing that their interests are being served by the status quo (Dyson and Brown 2005).

As we can see with the example of the young women above, it is possible to see her as 'pathologizing' her background and, by implication, herself. But to do so is to override the somewhat canny analysis of poverty-level serial monogamy that she presents. Instead of overriding the interpretations of situations given by participants, Hill Collins (2000) offers four criteria for interpreting truth and knowledge claims. These are: 1) primacy of lived experience; 2) dialogue; 3) an ethics of care; and 4) an ethics of responsibility. This framework privileges lived experience, emotion, empathy and values rooted in personal expressiveness, rather than the researchers' framework (Edwards *et al.* 2002: 25). In the way advocated by Collins, the researcher – who is also a kind of 'moral inquirer' – builds a collaborative, reciprocal, trusting, mutually accountable relationship with those studied (Denzin *et al.* 2006). In this way, perhaps, it is possible to retain a suitable level of fidelity to the people involved in the research and to the possibility of doing research that is valuable in itself on theoretical and epistemological grounds.

From cases to theories: Making small-scale interpretative research count

In qualitative and interpretive research it is often possible to make theoretically significant statements about the topic of enquiry on the basis of what might appear to be relatively little data. There is, however, something special about individual cases that do not fit the expectations derived from theories, and small-scale research is often extremely useful when the researchers want to extend theorizing in new directions. Case studies are used in a range of social science disciplines involving people and programmes (Ragin 1992, Stake 1995, Yin 2003). Case studies can be used as teaching or instructional aids too (Stake 1995,

2000); as a form of record-keeping in order to facilitate practice (Yin 2003), as well as a strategy to solve practical problems (Hammersley and Gomm; *et al.* 2000, Luck *et al.* 2006). Case studies are used to explore, describe or explain the case of interest and facilitate the development of context-rich knowledge and understandings about everyday life events (Yin 2003). Case studies are also used to extensively study or analyse relatively common or mundane phenomena. Equally they are valuable for understanding events, social activities and occurrences that happen very rarely (Langford 2001). In educational settings, case studies can be valuable for situations where the phenomenon of interest is interdependent with, or enmeshed in, the context of the study (Yin 2003, Luck *et al.* 2006). The actions of everyday people doing things are often enmeshed in larger scale social processes. As Bourdieu says, 'the cognitive structures which social agents implement in their practical knowledge of the social world are internalized, "embodied" social structures' (Bourdieu 1986: 468). Thus, as Stake (2000) claims, case studies have the capacity to offer purposive, situational or interrelated descriptions of phenomena which connect practical complex events to theoretical abstractions (Stake 2000).

Pickering (2006) deploys this kind of approach in seeking to understand the changing experiences of people who have taken up teaching in higher education. This fits in with the UK's policy agenda of attempting to provide training for educators in higher education. However, we are still at an early stage of understanding what happens to lecturers and students during this process. Pickering's paper is based upon the reflections of several novice teachers in higher education on their experiences. As one engineer said, as a result of his experiences in his first year lecturing: 'There are many things which have been a surprise to me . . . I've realized that there is quite a lot about my subject that I don't understand (Peter, interview, late in the study)' (Pickering 2006: 327).

Pickering adds that Peter had begun to consider that, as he tried to explain the fundamentals of his subject to the students, this exposed the limitations of his own understanding of those concepts and issues. While a student himself, or as a practitioner, it might have been sufficient to apply formulaic knowledge, for example, in relation to design problems. This did not suffice in teaching it to others. As he went on to say:

> Because I've had to simplify it to explain it, because again coming back to the idea that there's a formula for everything, that there's a prescribed way of doing a design exercise, you don't necessarily need to understand the fundamentals for that . . . But if you're teaching it you can't say that . . . You should go back to the fundamentals and make sure the students are with you on it (Peter, interview, late in the study). (Pickering, 2006: 327)

This has a number of important implications, too, for how we conceive of expertise and how people represent knowledge. Peter had found that, even as an expert, he found it challenging to understand and explain fundamental aspects of his discipline. Indeed, as one becomes an expert it may well be that the knowledge one deploys is less declarative and more likely to be implicit (Dunphy and Williamson 2004). Peter was discovering that the previous formulation of his knowledge base was no longer entirely plausible in the pedagogic context. Also important was the sheer volume of work involved in keeping up with the teaching programme in one's first year of teaching. This was characterized by another of her informants, Simon, as 'just keeping your head above water' (Pickering 2006: 327).

A further difficulty faced by the people involved in Pickering's study concerned the task of interesting, involving and motivating students. The lack of interest shown by students in the teaching programmes for which they were responsible was dispiriting for new lecturers. Where it could be achieved, a 'dialogue' between lecturer and students was symbiotic and, as Simon indicated, seemed to make a difference to the extent to which the informants felt they could affect student learning:

> I just ask the question what am I doing this for when a lot of these people are not interested? Why am I bothering? You know

> especially when you put a lot of effort into it it's frustrating. No it doesn't sit comfortably with me that I'm doing this and half the people are sat there and they just look bored (Simon, interview, late in the study). (Pickering 2006: 328)

What was also intriguing and potentially significant from the point of view of understanding the process of becoming a university teacher was that, particularly in the short term, Pickering's informants derived a good deal of support from their immediate colleagues within their particular disciplinary specialism. This offers the opportunity for such a community to become systematically involved in the development of new lecturers and may be especially valuable given that many now find the higher education environment 'inhospitable' (Knight and Trowler 2000). This affords some important links with other literature on learning and the notion of communities of practice (Wenger 1998). In a university context this is also raised by Lueddeke (2003) as encouraging a focus on teaching and learning in higher education, since this will facilitate collaborative development and an exchange of views on issues 'that really do matter to staff and students' (Hutchings 2000, Lueddeke 2003: 224).

Thus, the milieu of learning is important in this view. Being able to observe colleagues at work, participate in the local work culture of practice, and the learning communities of the workplace all enhance the 'zone of proximal development'. Thus, advice to learn by watching more experienced colleagues (Patvardhan 2005), or the literature on the value of learning communities in workplaces (Eraut 1994, 2000) and the value attached to informal learning all address this issue. Communitarian, milieu-based learning is therefore important, as well as anything that can be formally learned in the classroom.

This also ties in with the notion of situated learning (Lave and Wenger 1991) and distributed cognition (Salomon 1993). A good deal of the study of learning has proceeded as if it involved individual cognitive processes which were 'possessed and residing in the heads of individuals' (Salomon 1993: xii). By contrast the study of distributed cognition has looked to:

> the tools and social relations 'outside' people's heads. They are not only sources of stimulation and guidance but are actually vehicles of thought . . . It is not just the 'person-solo' who learns, but the 'person-plus'; the whole system of interrelated factors.
>
> (*ibid.*: xiii)

In other words, people think in and through relationships with others and use a variety of socially and culturally available tools. Different cognitions will emerge in different situations. Therefore, Pickering (2006) suggests that the best way to learn about the teaching of a subject would be among one's own discipline group. The significance of the informants' teaching encounters would also suggest that these would be central to the teaching practice and to development and the inclusion of students in the notion of communities of practice (Trigwell and Shale 2004).

The work of novice teachers in communities of practice also recollects the work of Lave and Wenger (1991) concerning how communities learn and expertise is passed from one generation of artisans to the next. At an early stage in many occupations, new entrants undertake a good deal of fetching, carrying and making refreshments – this is called by Lave and Wenger 'legitimate peripheral participation'. Things are not quite the same in higher education teaching; nevertheless, this informal process of 'soaking up' the skills and practice of more experienced practitioners is an important way of learning about professional life, and one which can be harnessed in training and pedagogy.

> Learners inevitably participate in communities of practitioners and . . . the mastery of knowledge and skill requires newcomers to move toward full participation in the sociocultural practices of a community. 'Legitimate peripheral participation' provides a way to speak about the relations between newcomers and old-timers, and about activities, identities, artefacts and communities of knowledge and practice. A person's intentions to learn are engaged and the meaning of learning is configured through the process of becoming a full participant in a sociocultural practice.

> This social process, includes, indeed it subsumes, the learning of knowledgeable skills. (Lave and Wenger 1991: 29)

Thus, case studies can be valuable in exploring the contours of hitherto unexplored social phenomena in education and elsewhere; and they can be valuable in linking the experiences, actions and learning processes of the people studies to broader understandings of the world. There was a time when the learning process was thought of and studied in largely individualized, cognitive terms. However, through observation of learners and the communities of practice into which they insinuate themselves, it has been possible to reformulate learning and the acquisition of skills as a social process that is enabled through participation in communities of practice. Thus, this kind of observation on a case-by-case basis can enable our theories, ideas and frameworks of understanding themselves to be challenged and reformulated.

As McDermott (in Murphy 1999:17) puts it:

> Learning traditionally gets measured as on the assumption that it is a possession of individuals that can be found inside their heads . . . [Here] learning is in the relationships between people. Learning is in the conditions that bring people together and organize a point of contact that allows for particular pieces of information to take on a relevance; without the points of contact, without the system of relevancies, there is not learning, and there is little memory. Learning does not belong to individual persons, but to the various conversations of which they are a part.

It is experiences like this which highlight the socially embedded nature of thinking and experience which have been responsible for the growth in popularity of social constructionist approaches in the social sciences over the last couple of decades. These represent a kind of paradigm in themselves, often loosely grouped together under the heading of 'social constructionism' which informs a great deal of interpretive enquiry in the social sciences.

Social constructionism and educational research

The focus of much social-constructionist scholarship has been concerned with discovering how individuals and groups participate jointly in the creation of their perceived reality. The hallmark of social constructionist work is that it involves examining how social phenomena are formulated, institutionalized and perhaps even made into tradition by humans. Taking its cue from Berger and Luckmann's book *The Social Construction of Reality* (1963), social realities are seen as an ongoing, dynamic process as people work together – or sometimes in opposition – to construct and reproduce reality by acting on their interpretations and their knowledge of it (Coulter 1979, Gergen 1985, Burr 1995). Most variants of social constructionism contend that what passes for reality is inextricably bound to human practices of meaning-making; a position indebted to Wittgenstein (1958) and Garfinkel (1967). Berger and Luckmann (1963) argue that human knowledge, including the most basic, taken-for-granted commonsense knowledge of everyday reality, is derived from and maintained by social interactions.

When people interact, they usually do so on the basis of an implicit understanding that their respective perceptions of reality are related and as they act upon this understanding their common knowledge of reality becomes reinforced. Shared meanings are constructed by people in their interactions with each other, and used as an everyday resource to interpret elements of their social and cultural lives. This is not to say that human beings always agree upon everything. Instead, within social constructionism, there is often an emphasis upon the multiplicity of interrelated, subjective and often oppositional understandings, each with their own inherent validity (Ussher 1999) that may compete for dominance in social situations.

Even though this commonsense knowledge is negotiated by people, through repetition it often comes to look remarkably solid. Human typifications, significations and institutions come to be presented as part of an 'objective reality'. 'It's the way it is', 'It's how we've always done it' and 'It stands to reason' are phrases that embody this sense of permanence and solidity about human affairs. It is in this sense that it can be said that reality is 'socially constructed'. In most versions of social constructionism, language is seen to play a pivotal role. Individual and collective realities are constructed in 'discourse', which can include speech, written texts, and socially intelligible gestures, that is actions sequences of behaviour. Research on discourse tries to uncover for critical scrutiny the ways in which speech, writing and action formulates distinctive versions of the world (Burman and Parker 1993, Potter and Wetherall 1995). It is a hermeneutic enterprise that is concerned with the process of interpretation.

Berger and Luckmann's (1963) contention that important aspects of shared human realities, including identity itself, were constructed through social processes, laid the ground for many further inquiries into how stories structured the world (Maines 1993, Gotham and Staples 1996). Viewed in this way, the discourse through which people construct their realities is to be regarded not as true or false, but instead as conforming to 'felicity conditions'; that is, it aims to be appropriate to the situation from the point of view of participants in the interaction (Ashworth *et al.* 2001).

To return to the education field . . . For an example of this process at work, let us consider the work of Phil Brown and his colleagues on what they called the 'social construction of graduate employability' (Brown *et al.* 2004, Brown 2005). On the face of it, if we were to take at their word announcements from government representatives and industrialists, we live in a fast-moving world of 'people in smart jobs, doing smart things, in smart ways, for smart money'. Moreover, the implication of so much encouragement to enter higher education is that this world is increasingly open to all rather than a few. A future in challenging, exciting and financially rewarding jobs designed for winners is presented in glossy corporate websites and brochures. They also convey an image of enlightened employers actively seeking to diversify their talent pool in those they recruit for fast-track management appointments.

Instead, say Brown *et al.* (2004), graduates are faced with a job market where degrees are declining in value and where employers often have little use for the 'skills' possessed by contemporary graduates. Instead, there seems to be a complex social and linguistic process at work where some graduates – especially those from elite institutions – are successful in presenting themselves in a particular way. As Brown (2005: 8) puts it:

> Personal capital involves packaging credentials, skills and charismatic qualities in ways that can be convincingly sold in the market for managerial and professional work. The 'hard' currency of credentials is insufficient to secure elite employment; as one employer noted, 'academic qualifications are the first tick in the box and then we move on. Today, we simply take them for granted.' Consequently, greater emphasis has been placed on 'soft currencies' including people skills, drive, self-confidence and self-reliance. Graduates can no longer capitalise on their cultural backgrounds and 'extracurricular' activities (i.e. university club captain; voluntary work; or extensive travel during a gap year) unless packaged in ways that demonstrate the personal qualities that meet the range of managerial competences organizations have benchmarked as indicative of elite employability. This 'economy of experience' has to be packaged as a *narrative* of employability that must be sold to employers.

So, as social constructionist approaches of the kind we have mentioned above would predict, there are a variety of strategies – often linguistic in nature – which people use to both present themselves as a suitable employee and, behind this, construct themselves through their university life as being the right kind of person. Significantly, Brown says that people have to package themselves in terms of a 'narrative'. Put crudely, narratives are the stories that people tell about their lives (Gray *et al.* 2005). As Prince called it: 'The recounting . . . of one or more real or fictitious events . . .' (Prince 1991: 58). Some would argue that this definition is incomplete and that a text should describe at least two events for it to be considered a narrative (Barthes 1982, Rimmon-Kenan 2002). Frid *et al.* (2000) add the importance of a point of view, and that this is what distinguishes narratives from stories: 'narrative is an account of events experienced by the narrator', while storytelling is 'the repeated telling or reading of a story by persons other than the narrator' (2000: 695). Paley and Eva (2005: 86) add more:

> What is required, we think, is the sense of one thing leading to another; the idea that something happened as a result of something else . . . In saying this, we are agreeing with another group of critics who argue, not only that a narrative must include reference to two or more events, but also that some of those events must be causally related.

Veteran qualitative researcher Denzin (1989: 37) provides the following definition:

> A 'narrative' is a story that tells a sequence of events that are significant for the narrator and his or her audience. A narrative as a story has a plot, a beginning, a middle and an end. It has an internal logic that makes sense to the narrator. A narrative relates events in a temporal, causal sequence. Every narrative describes a sequence of events that have happened.

Narrators render the events of their lives meaningful by linking them to other life-events, through links forged between these and the general experience of a broader sweep of humanity, and by providing temporal ordering of these events (Hydén 1997). Importantly, in the light of the concerns about culture and context, narratives formulate the context for human activity, which might be temporal, spatial, interpersonal or societal (Clandinin and Connelly 2000).

We will be exploring the possibilities of narrative approaches in educational studies in Chapters 4 and 5 as a counterpoint to the role of experiments and quantitative approaches in the educational field. However, they represent an appropriate note on which to end this chapter because, in a sense, it has been largely about storytelling. First, the stories about the research process itself and how they shift as paradigms change, and subsequently, as we have explored various ways in which researchers have sought to make sense of the kinds of things that people say and do in or around the post-compulsory education system. It is a theme or motif which we will revisit later in this story of how we can make sense of social experience in post-compulsory education.

In conclusion, this chapter has reviewed some of the developments in the philosophy of science that help to put the differing strands of research in higher education in context. The idea of paradigms and paradigm shifts has been explored as a means of illuminating how different research traditions have proliferated. However, unlike the paradigm changes that have been seen in the field of physics, there are a number of different paradigms co-existing in social science research of which educational enquiry is a particular branch.

What makes it more confusing in the social sciences is that there is sometimes a sense of tension or even open hostility between the different camps. Moreover, in the field of higher education this is also tied in with the sorts of ideas people have about what they would like to see universities become.

Interpretative approaches in the social sciences have a great deal to offer those who seek to understand educational phenomena. Yet it is only relatively recently that many researchers have applied these methods to understanding the experience of people entering the higher education system and absorbing the leaning experiences it has to offer. So far, many of these alignments of research that have emphasized the students' experience have tended to also emphasize the first-hand, hyper-authentic voices of the students as research participants, without placing them in any more rigorous critical framework that allows us to take stock of their experiences. Thus, occasionally work can appear naïve with regard to the organizational and political constraints dictating how rapidly institutions can change.

In the light of this, we would like to plead for a flexible, epistemologically nuanced caution in interpreting qualitative research in higher education and alert the reader to be prepared to undertake their own critical analysis when confronted with new forms of enquiry or new results. Moreover, there are important questions relating to the links between the conversations researchers have with research participants and the grander social structures and processes which researchers take them to exemplify, such as class, gender and racial oppression. A researcher's case may be weakened if these are assumed too glibly.

Of course, as we have shown, the accounts from individual research participants and researchers can be linked to more general theories about what happens in the educational arena. Understanding people getting to grips with the job of lecturing, or contrasting their early life experience with experiences and aspirations as a young adult, requires some intriguing analytical manoeuvres and it is these that we will be getting to grips with in the next chapter.

4

Philosophies of research in education: Knowledge in education and knowledge of education

Introduction: Thinking about the process of knowing in higher education

This chapter will take the insights gained from the previous two chapters and critically interrogate some of the major trends in educational enquiry. The aim of the chapter is to give the reader a sense of how we come to know about educational phenomena as researchers and practitioners, and we will explore some of the ideas and assumptions involved in doing so, with particular emphasis on how inquiries in higher education are undertaken.

Understanding the phenomena encountered in higher education has become particularly pressing due to the recent rapid expansion of this particular sphere of human activity. In all developed nations there has been a substantial expansion of educational provision throughout the twentieth century, but as Nash (2003) notes, this has been accomplished while leaving social differentials in school attainment and post-compulsory educational participation virtually untouched (Shavit and Blossfield 1993).

The question of how educational inequality is sustained and how it could be ameliorated has dominated many research agendas in educational studies. Policy-makers have sought to uncouple the link between social class and educational attainment and to maximize 'social inclusion'. They have been frustrated by a complex array of processes which the sociology of education struggles to understand in its explanatory narratives. Coleman (1991) has set the agenda for the field in speaking of 'inequality of educational opportunity' as being the key issue behind differences or inequalities in educational attainment. The causes of this are likely to be multiple, and as we shall see later there has been a good deal of research seeking to statistically isolate and determine the relative weights of discrete variables which may be involved.

However, as Nash (2003) argues, the most influential sociological theories of how difference and inequality is sustained in education take little from statistical investigations, other than that inequality is a constant finding, and argue that schools are, perhaps inevitably, 'agents of social and cultural reproduction' (Nash 1997). Despite the stubborn inequalities still evident in the social composition of the student body, widening participation has had a considerable effect on the higher education system. There are now much higher numbers of people entering higher education and therefore greater numbers of people from groups which, previously, did not usually access higher education. This fundamental demographic shift is bringing with it a unique set of difficulties, as hitherto separate ideas, values and styles of life are brought together. Changes are being wrought not only in the applicants, but are being urged with vigour upon higher education institutions. Conceptual shifts have accompanied these demographic and policy changes. There are reconfigurations of what it means to be a student and what higher education entails, as well as attempts to reformulate the very nature of higher education institutions themselves. Some of these reconfigurations are changing the conceptual landscape of thinking about education, often with little debate or effective challenge.

Despite these blindspots in grasping what higher education has become, there has been a corresponding expansion in research on the process of higher education itself. Approaches which emphasize social processes, cultural capital and *habitus* contrast with others that emphasize the internal psychometric properties of the students and the measurement of motivation, aptitude and achievement. As we have seen in Chapter 1, evidence-based initiatives in education have tended to prioritize a model of research quality based on randomized, controlled trials in medical research, yet the suitability or epistemological status of these methods in education has rarely been unpacked and systematically questioned. Later, in considering evidence-based or evidence-informed practice in the study of education, we will discuss some of the difficulties in adopting an experimental approach. It is important, in this context, to consider some of the threats to the validity and reliability of experimental data as well as the problems that arise when practitioners try to generalize the results of such trials from one setting to another.

Another important spur to the study of educational processes and activities in post-compulsory education lies in the desire to establish some system of training or accreditation for teachers in colleges and universities. The hope has been that new generations of better-trained lecturers will gradually improve learning and teaching experiences to meet the challenge of increased student numbers, and enhance the quality of the student experience in higher education. This is particularly urgent in the UK, because universities are setting great store by their position in the various higher education guides published by national newspapers and the results of surveys of student opinion.

Developing knowledge, developing teachers

In light of these initiatives to develop university and college staff as teachers, it is particularly important to understand what is going on when we think about the teaching and learning experience. A good deal of professional development for staff draws upon the ideas of reflective practice which have been used for some time in healthcare. Fostering reflective practice in lecturers is an idea inspired by Schön's work (1983, 1987) and forms a significant part of the approach taken on courses for novice lecturers, at least in terms of their espoused theory (Ecclestone 1996).

In adopting this kind of approach to professional development, educators are implicitly adopting an epistemological stance towards teaching and learning. Schön's idea of a reflective practitioner is rooted in a critique of the technical-rationalist approach to professional practice. It gained a substantial following in nursing as a way of thinking about the intuitive and interpersonal aspects of the craft, rather than an instrumental approach that determines a single 'right' way for professionals to conduct learning in different circumstances regardless of context. In Schon's formulation, the idea of reflective practice assumes that skilled professional practice is built around a kind of artistry and that to become a better practitioner, one needs to undertake a careful examination of the artistry involved. The best measure of that artistry is how one ventures into unknown territory: 'that is, the competence by which practitioners actually handle indeterminate zones of practice' (Schön 1987: 13).

Becoming a reflective practitioner involves developing the ability to think about one's practice in intelligent ways and thereby developing the level of artistry, which requires hard work and diligence: 'The student cannot be *taught* what he [*sic*] needs to know, but he can be *coached*' (Schön 1987: 17). Schön saw his work as representing an extension of John Dewey's (1859–1952) generative thinking about the educational process. Dewey was an adherent of a view called 'instrumentalism' which maintained that truth is an instrument used by human beings to solve their problems, and that educational advances occur through the acquisition of particular kinds of experiences. From the learner's point of view, education looks like this:

> He [*sic*] has to see on his own behalf and in his own way the relations between means and methods employed and results achieved. Nobody else can see for him, and he can't see just by being 'told', although the right kind of telling may guide his seeing and thus help him to see what he needs to see. (Dewey 1974: 151)

This kernel of thinking, as Trowler *et al.* (2005) note, remains at the core of almost all higher education teachers' educational programmes.

Therefore, an important strand of thinking in developing knowledge of education and knowledge in education involves exploring the inner worlds of the teacher and learner. In order to understand what this is based upon, let us take a step back to reconnoitre the territory of phenomenology, a source of inspiration for many of these trends.

Phenomenology and phenomenography

Phenomenology originated with the work of Brentano (1838–1917), Husserl (1859–1938) and Heidegger (1889–1976), who sought to obtain an accurate description and understanding of lived human experience. That is, from the perspective of an individual's consciousness, directed or intended towards objects in the world (intentionality) – without being contaminated by assumptions about their 'objective reality'. It does this by 'bracketing' out the beliefs, attitudes and, indeed, prejudices of the researcher(s) that may unduly shape the description of whatever lived human experience is being accounted for. Examination of a person's subjective viewpoint or consciousness – something which is often discounted or taken for granted – may be extended to include others and how they interrelate–intersubjectivity. Whether the focus is on the subjective or intersubjective realm, phenomenology seeks to provide an account of lived experiences or the 'life world' of individuals. As a rather heterogeneous approach within an interpretativist tradition, phenomenology seeks to advance understanding of how consciousness and objective phenomena interact in the interpretation and, at times, construction of social life. Mental and psychological acts such as thinking, feeling and perceiving are used to describe and understand human experiences. Within this tradition there is a strong belief that the experience itself must be subject to systematic investigation, and the underlying assumption of the phenomenologist is '. . . that human experiences can be catalogued and described in order to learn how we get meaning from our experiences' (Eichelberger 1989).

In other words, phenomenology examines the cognitive activity at the heart of human society. For example, if we were to study any given phenomenon in higher education, we would be doing so by examining accounts of those experiencing it. We might investigate what is the lived, subjective experience of undertaking a particular learning exercise, or educational phenomenon, such as the reticence of students to speak in class discussions, the process of engaging in group work and what it feels like to be assessed on presentations. In addition, our descriptions as practitioners, researchers or students may uncover different aspects of the educational process that are novel or hitherto understudied.

The importance of phenomenology as an approach and the range of influence it has had is considerable. The interpretativist or constructivist paradigm in social research grew out of Edmund Husserl's phenomenology. Wilhelm Dilthey's (1833–1911) and other German philosophers' study of interpretative understanding called hermeneutics was inspired by similar concerns (Eichelberger 1989, Mertens 2005: 12). Like phenomenology, interpretativist and constructivist approaches aim to understand 'the world of human experience' (Cohen and Manion 1994: 36), and are founded on the assumption that important aspects of human social realities are 'socially constructed' (Mertens 2005: 12). These kinds of inquiries prioritize the meanings human beings singly or collectively attribute to things in the world. Schutz (1899–1959) did a great deal to bring phenomenology out of the sphere of philosophy and into the realm of social science. Schutz (1962: 59) said:

> The world of nature, as explored by the natural scientist, does not 'mean' anything to the molecules, atoms and electrons. But the observational field of the social scientist – social reality – has a specific meaning and reference structure for the human beings living, acting and thinking within it.

Interpretative or constructivist researchers who are informed by the legacy of phenomenology tend to foreground the 'participants' views of the situation being studied' (Creswell 2003: 8) and focus also, in a reflexive fashion, upon their own impact on the research situation and the effects of their own background and experiences. Researchers in this tradition do not generally begin with a theory; instead they 'generate or inductively develop a theory or pattern of meanings' (Creswell 2003: 9) through the research process itself. The contemporary phenomenological researcher is most likely to rely on qualitative data collection methods and analysis or a combination of both qualitative and quantitative methods (mixed methods). Quantitative data may be utilized so as to support or expand upon qualitative data or effectively deepen the description.

There has been a great deal of interest in the investigation of the perceptions and cognitive operations that enable people to explore the world around them, avoid danger and solve problems. Within psychology, through the latter years of the twentieth century, there was an important strand of work that sought to elicit people's descriptions of their cognitive operations as they solved problems. This 'verbal protocol analysis' (Ericsson and Simon 1993) has been deployed in many studies of thinking, product testing, problem-solving and, increasingly, in education (Renkl 1997).

In the educational field, this interest in the processes of learning and reflection is important for two major reasons. First, because it relates to the reflective practitioner agenda we have mentioned above, which can be found in many attempts to develop staff as effective educators. Second, because it is believed to be a useful tool in exploring how learners learn and the diverse psychosocial factors involved. Thus it is of value in finding out how people might be enabled to learn more effectively.

These interests have condensed into a tradition of enquiry called phenomenography, which we shall consider in some detail because it is particularly aligned with the educational enterprise. Within this tradition, which now stretches back over a quarter of a century, some of the most influential research on the learning process in higher education has been undertaken by Ference Marton and his colleagues at the University of Gothenburg (Marton and Saljo 1976a, 1976b; Fransson 1977; Svensson 1977). Marton's work has covered issues such as student's conceptions of learning, their struggles with specific learning tasks, teaching and assessment. These factors, along with the subject matter of their studies itself, is believed to have a significant impact on learning outcomes. The original work was undertaken when the subsection of the population entering university was much smaller and were likely to have followed an intensive academic curriculum from an early stage in their educational careers.

With a more diverse student body entering higher education than was the case a generation ago, a considerable challenge is presented to university teachers in creating appropriate learning experiences. Recently, phenomenography has been applied in other nations, such as Australia and in the UK (e.g. Entwistle and Entwistle 1991, Prosser and Trigwell 1999); and in disciplines such as politics (Cloonan and Davies 1998), physics and biology (Hegarty-Hazel and Prosser 1991a, 1991b), medicine and psychology (Lonka and Lindblom-Ylanne 1996), history (Newton and Newton 1997, 1998; Gunn 2003), geography (Bradbeer *et al.* 2004) and mathematics (Crawford *et al.* 1994, 1998).

Phenomenography has been defined as 'the description of some examined phenomenon' (Kroksmark 1987: 226–7) with human experience as its object. It is described by Marton (1986: 31) as:

> a research method for mapping the qualitatively different ways in which people experience, conceptualize, perceive and understand various aspects of, and phenomena in, the world around them.

It is focused on ways of experiencing different phenomena, ways of seeing them and knowing about them, and encompasses the variation of experience and the architecture of variation. Differing experiences and understandings are characterized in terms of description. As Webb (1997) notes, phenomenography differs from phenomenology in that it considers only the 'second order' or conceptual thoughts of people. Phenomenography attempts to aggregate 'modes of experience . . . forms of thought' (Marton 1981: 181) into a limited number of categories. Phenomenographers do not claim to study 'what is there' in the world (reality) but they do claim to study 'what is there' in people's conceptions of the world.

The dominant method for collecting the data is the individual interview, carried out as a dialogue, where the interviewee is encouraged to reflect on previously unthematized aspects of the phenomenon being examined. Interviews are transcribed and analysis carried out on transcripts. The units of analysis are different ways of experiencing the phenomena. Marton (1986: 38) describes 'pure' phenomenography as 'how people conceive of various aspects of their reality'. Marton and Saljo (1976: 113) define the research object of phenomenographic research in the following terms: 'The unit of phenomenographic research – a way of experiencing something – [. . .] is an internal relationship between the experiencer and the experienced.'

Phenomenography seeks to generalize, so while accounts of individuals' experiences provide the raw material, the categories of description which the researcher derives from this draw upon aspects of the experience of many individuals. Marton and Saljo suggest three key criteria for a set of descriptive categories derived from phenomenographic analysis:

i) individual categories should stand in relation to the phenomenon of the investigation so that each category tells us something distinct about a particular way of experiencing the phenomenon;
ii) categories have to stand in a logical relationship with one another, a relationship that is frequently hierarchical;
iii) the system should be parsimonious . . . [with] . . . as few categories as is feasible and reasonable to capture the critical variation. (Marton and Saljo 1997: 125)

The results of this derivation of categories are typically then interpreted at a collective level, without relating a particular way of understanding something to a specific individual or to groups of individuals. In this framework 'individual learning is interpreted, or defined, as acquiring the capacity to see something in a qualitatively new way. Learning, understood in this way, is shaped both by the learners and the phenomena they study' (Berglund 2004: 66).

As with phenomenology itself, the process of undertaking phenomenographic analysis entails acknowledging and managing the researcher's own subjectivity:

> The researcher withholds theories and prejudices when he/she interprets the individuals' conceptions being investigated. The reduction does not mean, however, that the researcher must or can bracket all previous experience of the object under consideration (Sandberg 1997: 209).

To add context to such an analysis, it is useful to ground the analysis on three different levels of the concept of context. The following account of context is from Berglund (2004: 71):

1. *The experienced context of the individual* describes the relationship between a phenomenon and its context. During a 'phenomenographic interview, some aspects of the phenomenon come into focus, while others remain in the background. The phenomenon is thus experienced against and interwoven with an experienced context, what we can refer to as the *experienced context of the individual*' (italics in original).
2. *The experienced context of the collective* describes the interplay between utterances of different individuals. 'When analysing the interviews, the researcher finds that light is shed on some utterance made by one interviewee by reading it against the background of the context deduced or assumed by the researcher from reading an interview extract by another interviewee. Switching between these two perspectives allows the researcher to let an aspect of a phenomenon as experienced by one participant interplay with an expression of an experienced context that originates from another participant.'
3. *The experienced context of the researcher* describes the researcher's relationship to the object of his/her research: 'it can be claimed that when engaged in a phenomenographic study on learning the researcher stands in the same relationship to the object of research as the learner stands to the object of learning. The object of research is embedded in a context,

> and this context can be said to be what lends meaning to the object.'

Thus, it is argued, through the deployment of these kinds of methods we can achieve the kind of analysis advocated by Entwistle (1984: 17):

> the method of qualitative analysis is distinctive, and exceptionally rigorous. It sets out to identify concepts which describe important differences in the ways in which students learn and study. The specific differences give rise to distinct categories and each category is defined, or delimited, in terms of those extracts from the interviews which together constitute its meaning . . . The procedure thus carries the 'hallmark' of scientific research, while not following the methods of the natural sciences.

This, then, is the manifest picture of the field. It has shown itself to be an attractive one for many who are seeking to formulate the problems of learning in researchable terms. However, as we might expect, there are some critical voices in the field who have pointed to limitations, and have highlighted underlying assumptions of the approach which may be difficult to sustain in practice.

Phenomenography's limits

Firstly, in terms of the overall position taken, Webb (1997: 198) notes that it is curiously domesticated and has no particular ambitions to push forward the more fundamental questions of values in education:

> Phenomenography appears to have no particular view of humanity and the social consequences of education. For example, it is not in any sense politically radical and no responsibility is placed upon lecturers to produce social reformers; to motivate transformative intellectuals; to argue the oppressive nature of education within an unequal society or to call for de-schooling.

One area where phenomenographic approaches do take sides is on the value of certain kinds of approaches and activities in learning. Webb notes that phenomenography has been linked to accounts of leaning which emphasize the contrast between 'deep' and 'surface' approaches. This means that it enjoys a ready alignment with ideas about learning and remembering from Craik and Lockhart (1972) and Gagne (1970). It therefore has some degree of assumed respectability as an intellectual enterprise. As this volume is intended to explore the theoretical and philosophical foundations of research enterprises, it might repay us to explore some of the assumptions which appear to run through this enterprise. There is a highly particular model of mind at work here. It is supposed that the significant elements of thinking, perceiving and problem solving are accessible to conscious inspection and elicitation. This is unlike some of the other approaches and findings in cognitive science originating around the same time, which stressed how much of the activity in question was not susceptible to conscious access and that where people's accounts were elicited they might turn out to be actively misleading. Nisbett and Wilson (1977: 246) concluded: 'In summary, it would appear that people may have little ability to report accurately on their cognitive processes.'

Phenomenography, like many other accounts based on techniques of enquiry as diverse as discourse analysis, interpretive phenomenological analysis and hermeneutics, also assumes sufficient homogeneity between individual and collective patterns of thought that we can meaningfully aggregate them together and construct a shared model. However, different people may arrive at answers in very different ways, and in a diverse learning environment where experiences and cultural problem-solving tools may differ dramatically, this may be a difficult assumption to sustain in practice.

Webb draws parallels between the way that phenomenography helps to construct a discourse about what is going on in learners' heads and the work of Foucault (e.g. 1972). Foucault saw knowledge not as coming from the natural world around us in any simple sense. For him, knowledge was always about power. It took power to impose a particular way of looking at the world, power to carve up nature into collectively intelligible human categories and power to enforce a particular way of looking inside ourselves to see the appropriate kinds of structures and processes. The luxuriant interior jungle, full of things like motivation, levels of processing, self-esteem, personal epistemological beliefs, emotional literacy and so on, has not been around for ever. As Rose (1990) points out, we see ourselves in this way because of the pervasiveness of psychological discourse in developed nations through the twentieth century. In the same sort of way, the means by which we grasp the 'truth' of teaching or learning is through spatially and historically situated discourse constructed in such a way as to encode dominant ways of understanding people and ways of seeing the world. As Webb (1997: 209–10) reminds us:

> The truth of the discourse is the truth of the power relationships of the discourse . . . We cannot, for example, 'reflect' on our teaching to produce some 'essential' truth about teaching, or an 'authentic' reflective practice. The very words themselves come from the discourse and what they come to mean in action is part of the discourse/practice. Power even moulds what we want to be: power shapes desire. Power as it is manifest in a discourse helps *make* the people of the discourse.

Thus, we are left in some doubt as to what the accounts produced by participants in studies mean. If we make the assumption that they reflect genuine accounts of cognitive processes involved in learning, thinking and developing expertise, then this can look naïve in the light of concerns about power and culture – these may reflect dominant ways of seeing the self or the psyche rather than any underlying operations undertaken in solving the problem.

In addition, in some phenomenographic work there is often a somewhat narrow conception of what the 'correct' answer is, so students and teachers are encouraged towards it. This reflects content considerations just as much as any level of processing that might have been achieved. For example, Taylor (1993) describes a phenomenographic approach to the process of learning the meaning of the concept of price in economics (Dahlgren and Marton 1978, Dahlgren 1984). The 'correct' understanding of price toward which the students were directed was as a function of supply and demand. Other conceptions of price were identified by the researchers as being somehow aberrant and wrong. For example, the idea that price might be influenced by the cost of production was a dispreferred conception, presumably indicating an insufficiently 'deep' understanding. However, as Webb (1997) points out, this latter idea corresponds to the labour theory of value in Marxist economics and was also common in early 'classical' economic theory. Thus, whether the conception is 'correct' or not is determined by the educators and researchers, and does not necessarily inhere in the idea itself. This example illustrates another aspect of the problem. The solutions that it is desirable to direct the students toward are defined in terms of content. Some answers are seen as better than others. This does not necessarily reflect a more or less 'deep' kind of processing. After all, classical economics can be learned superficially and Marxist economics learned deeply. The identification of the preferred learning outcomes do not necessarily reflect the superiority of the cognitive processes of the proficient 'deep' learner, but lie in the values and interpretation of the historically and socially located researcher.

These kinds of concerns about what people's reflections, cogitations and introspections mean also pertain to the idea of the reflective practitioner whom we met earlier. This idea is likewise one which has been subject to some debate or criticism (Trowler and Cooper 2002: 234–5). The term 'reflective practitioners' tends to permeate professional development programmes for lecturers. Ecclestone (1996) argues that it has become simply 'mantric theory' (Ball 1994), a theoretical device that has lost its meaning because it has come to encompass such a diverse range of practices, ideologies and activities. It has come to obscure rather than clarify:

> theory can also work to provide comforting and apparently stable identities for academics in an increasingly slippery world . . . Too often . . . theory becomes no more than a mantric reaffirmation of

> belief rather than a tool for exploration and for thinking otherwise. Such mantric uses of theories typically involve little more than a naming of spaces (Ball 1994 in Ecclestone 1996: 152)

Other authors have also suggested that the 'reflective practitioner' label may be problematic. Eraut (1994) and Wellington and Austin (1996) argue that there is a need to distinguish between different types of reflection and reflective practice. Bleakley (1999) identifies that there are several differing and incompatible assumptions about the nature of knowledge or underlying epistemologies underpinning the idea of reflective practice. For example, despite Schön's interest in the 'artistry' of professional practice, this aspect has been underdeveloped, while the more rationalistic angles, where novice practitioners are infused with knowledge and are led towards reflective practice by the experts, underlies a good deal of the work. Boud *et al.* (1998) identify a number of fatal problems with the concept, especially the fact that the nature and use of reflective practice is highly context-dependent. They also highlight the way that, in some schemes, reflective practice proceeds as if there were a set of rules that one had to follow and, in others, a degree of personal disclosure was encouraged that was potentially upsetting. Brookfield (1995) emphasizes the need to engage in critical reflection, yet the way that this requires a consistent and systematic approach to unearthing and scrutinising the assumptions underlying educational practices is often unmet, despite its headline presence in teaching materials for new lecturers.

In making sense of research about higher education, it is important to be critically aware of some of the implicit work that goes on to make the processes we study intelligible to researchers and the communities of interest who make up the research-reading audience. Nature does not take on shape and form all by itself in educational research. It is often laboriously and painstakingly conjured into being through diligent scientific work.

This is not to say that we can make up any kind of data we want. Research, however we conceptualize it, often involves a meticulous process of anchoring our account of the world to the data we have captured from it. The experiences of students and staff in post-compulsory education are not a primordial wilderness: much as the Garden of Eden was seen by Mediaeval theologians, it is carefully cultivated and under control. The notion of higher education itself is constructed in and through research. Researchers punctiliously formulate the problems, work from theoretically informed models and draw upon tacit theories about what happens and what matters in the higher education field.

Tacit theories: The study of gender in higher education scholarship

The idea of tacit theories and how they inform the formulation of the object of study is particularly conspicuous when we look at the way gender has been dealt with in the higher education and widening participation literature. It is to this we will now turn. This will enable us to explore the generative models of men and women, which animate the higher education literature; and the paradigms of gender difference, which trammel the lines of enquiry, help to interpret results, suggest explanations and foreclose questions of social identity for the research participants.

There is by now a substantial body of work regarding gender and education, much of it pertaining to women's experiences of higher education (Edwards 1993, Pascall and Cox 1993a, 1993b). Many of the groups of research participants involved are non-traditional students or women who are disadvantaged in some way (Tett 2000). There has been comparatively little exploration of men's experience of higher education *per se* (Maynard and Pearsall 1994) or even of the more privileged or 'traditional' women students. Much of the work regarding women's experience uses qualitative, interpretative approaches and descriptions of experience are a characteristic feature of this work. The work is often based on biographical or narrative approaches; with a particular kind of feminist interpretation of experience being common. As we shall show, they offer a simplistic variant of feminism, whose liberatory potential has been mitigated and which offers a somewhat static notion of gender differences, often on the basis of very small datasets. Studies have often sought to identify a typical 'woman's experience' in higher education, replete with the disadvantage, oppression and discrimination which are seen as somehow inevitably consequent upon their sex.

In doing this, researchers often had to look quite hard to find consistent gender differences, although a number of authors have attempted to characterize the distinctly gendered experiences of students undertaking higher education (Pascall and Cox 1993a, 1993b; Kehily 1995; Britton and Baxter 1999). Studies exploring the experiences of women undertaking access to higher education courses have also been carried out (Reay *et al.* 2002, Reay 2003).

Much of the work conducted in the 1990s and early twenty-first century that concentrated on women's experience of higher education often treated 'women' as an homogenous group with a common set of experiences, interests and ways of interpreting the world, whose experience was unproblematically related to gender. Thus, despite the feminist ambitions of much of this work, it was at the same time pervaded by a rather crude essentialism, and reproduced commonsensical gender categories. Sometimes one even gets the sense that some of this work is in the spirit of John Gray's popular *Men are from Mars, Women are from Venus* self-help volumes, where caricatures of men and women go on dates, have arguments (Gray 1992, 1995) and are disinclined to step outside their preformulated sex roles. The literature which we are speaking of here could easily be thought of as 'Mars and Venus go to college'.

The reproduction of commonsensical gender differences in literature on the higher education experience – even in the more sophisticated work – is in contrast to a number of strands of recent research and theory concerning gender. This attempts to account for the flexibility with which people can assume particular points of view, draw on different repertoires and adapt to their circumstances. In fields outside higher education research, a number of dissenting trends have emerged in gender scholarship. For example, one strand of contemporary scholarship draws upon Butler (1990a) who argued that gender was a kind of 'performative'. That is, it is a statement, a story or it is bringing something into being through a display of gendered behaviour. In this view, the speaker is knowingly assembling an identity as a man or a woman. Butler's (1990b) work on gender stresses pluralities among women, suggesting that positing a 'specifically feminine' sphere of identity presumes a spurious universality among them. When Butler (1990a) conceived of gender as a 'performative', she saw it as bringing social identity into being. Describing the hardship of looking after children, or the satisfaction of career success, is not simply to describe a fact of male or female experience, it is to do with how the speaker is knowingly assembling an identity as a man or woman. Butler argues that it is the act of performing gender that constitutes who we are. The belief in stable gender identities and gendered experiences of education is, Butler might argue, compelled by social sanction. This offers a challenge to more deterministic gender thinking. Yet there appears little scope for this kind of flexibility or adaptability in the relatively essentialist notions of gender exhibited in much scholarship on gender and higher education.

Much literature on higher education experience claims that males and females inhabit distinct gendered realms. Although later literature often introduces the effects of class and race, it is consistently concluded that succeeding in higher education and thus achieving upward social mobility, is particularly difficult for working-class women (Reay *et al.* 2002). Some research on women's experience of higher education has found that higher education actually challenges gender inequalities (Pascall *et al.* 1993a). Many studies of educational experience have drawn upon Bourdieu's term *habitus* to describe the orientations and values regarding education, for example in explaining the difficulty of working-class students in adapting to higher education (James 1995, Reay 2003).

Kehily (1995) maintained that a person's gender is an overdetermining factor in their life experiences and life chances and informs the kinds of self-narratives they construct. In much research on gender and higher education, differences in the narratives of men and women are stressed (Britton and Baxter 1999). Pascall and Cox (1993a, 1993b) saw the 'instrumental' orientation as male and 'self-fulfilment' as female. Reay's (2003) mature working-class women students were undertaking education for education's sake, rather than to attain the qualification. Britton and Baxter (1999) concede that a dichotomous approach over-simplifies gender, but argue that the discourse of the reflexive self is based on male experience. They believe it is based on a highly individualistic conception of self that does not adequately represent women's experience. Reay's (2003) working-class women students experienced problems in undergoing the process of individualization. The idea of credentialism – the need for formal recognition to validate and further a career – was found in Britton and Baxter's (1999) study in two middle-class women. The idea of self-transformation was found by Britton and Baxter to only apply to men. In their study, this focuses on changes in the self and identity as a catalyst for returning to education

Developing complexity: Towards a situated concept of gender in higher education

More recent work on gender and pre-higher education courses/ higher education has presented more complex analyses. Although recent work is more sophisticated, significant gender differences are nevertheless described, albeit intersecting with factors such as social class and ethnicity (Reay *et al.* 2002, Reay 2003). Some work has questioned whether women can formulate their identities in terms of the 'reflexive self' (a mode of being wherein the individual can consciously construct self and identity) in the same way as men (Britton and Baxter 1999, Reay 2003). According to Britton and Baxter (1999) the idea of the reflexive self was a repertoire exclusively deployed by men. Central to much of the research into gender and higher education are questions concerning identity in contemporary Western societies.

Some approaches have tried to integrate notions of structural constraint with an emphasis on flexibility and contingency. Britton and Baxter (1999: 179) see education as the 'key site for the construction of identity'. They use the idea of the 'reflexive self' (Beck

1992) and view the task of becoming a mature student as a 'continuous process of identity construction' (Britton and Baxter 1999: 180). They draw out common cultural themes from students' narratives and define four narrative types, these being gendered representations. Britton and Baxter attempt to 'recognise women's different experience' since 'men and women may not have access to the same repertoire of narratives through which to make sense of their lives' (1999: 183). They emphasize that the 'dominant cultural narrative of self . . . [is] . . . based on a highly individualistic conception of self which does not adequately represent women's experience' (1999: 183). The idea of a reflexive self is argued to be something that is peculiar to men's experience.

Reay (2003: 314) argues that although working-class women 'do not escape processes of individualisation, they are positioned very differently in relation to them' and observes that 'the costs of individualisation were greater for the mature working-class women in my sample than they were for the vast majority of their middle-class counterparts'.

The concept of the reflexive self has arguably become more important in the context of modernity. Reflexive self-awareness provides the individual with the opportunity to construct self-identity without restrictive tradition and culture, which previously created relatively rigid boundaries to the options for self-understanding. Reflexive selves are constantly revising and reforming themselves in the light of new information or circumstances (Giddens 1990: 38). By identifying women as being excluded from a 'reflexive self' narrative, much of the existing literature on gender and higher education perhaps underplays the degree of reflexive agency that women may exhibit. Researchers have focused on the ways in which feminine experience and consciousness is overdetermined by circumstances. Tett's (2000: 184) participants described their experiences in a way that reflects 'how they construct feminine and masculine identities, which are not static but are historically and spatially situated and evolving'. Although Tett suggests that students could think reflexively about their experiences of education she nevertheless claims that 'gender was an important force in differentiating the way that they described their life experiences' (2000: 185). Tett described her women participants as saying they were 'held back' in their education because of their communities' expectations of appropriate activities for girls.

In the literature, women tend to be presented as being restricted by structural constraints affecting their life chances and even the ways in which they can conceive of themselves. They are perceived to see the entry into education as a result of 'opportunities' made available as a result of some outside agency, and are often perceived to have little sense of career development other than an instrumental sense that qualifications might be advantageous. Reay's (2003) image differs here, showing women with a strong sense of wanting to contribute to the community once they have achieved their qualification.

The findings from such research have important implications for how we think about identity in relation to the higher education experience. Returning to Butler – a writer who emphasizes change, performance and the flexibility of human identity – we can see how this contrasts with a good deal of what has been written about the higher education experience and gender. A good deal of the material we have reviewed, by contrast, formulates an account of men and women and gendered identity which assumes that masculine and feminine genders will inevitably be built, by culture, upon 'male' and 'female' bodies, making their destinies, their consciousness and the mode of engagement with higher education inescapable. This picture allows little room for choice, difference or resistance, and under-theorizes the resourceful work that people do to gain some sense of autonomy in their particular niche in the social system. Moreover, in places it positions women as somehow passively waiting for 'opportunities' to be granted to them by structures, systems and people which themselves remain to be persuaded by widening access initiatives. The picture presented is not one of gender identity which is actively reformulating itself and solving problems, but of an identity which is somehow passively disclosable through the medium of interviews and focus group discussions.

Thus, the question of how we know about other human beings, their means of solving problems, their educational experiences and their lives is a central one to the theory and practice of educational enquiry.

The measurement of pedagogic phenomena: The construction of human kinds in university studies

A further noteworthy strand in the study of educational phenomena concerns the measurability of the phenomena in higher education. There are a large number of variables susceptible to this treatment. It is from the assiduous collection of various kinds of data like this that we gain an impression of rates of participation, whether widening access policies are working, whether different kinds of teaching methods are more effective than others or whether attitudes and orientations on the part of students are related to their success in the system.

Thus, it is statistics about participation rates that enables Modood (2006) to draw our attention to the fact that most ethnic minority groups in the UK are achieving a significantly higher rate of participation amongst their young adults than are the white British majority. Following on from this, he discusses the encouragement and value attached to education in many families who have migrated to the UK which may be responsible for a noticeably higher participation rate in some minority groups, such as those whose families came from India or Africa. Even groups who appear particularly disadvantaged in the UK, such as those who hail from Bangladesh or Pakistan, are placing a higher proportion of their young people in higher education than are the Caucasian majority, again, possibly because of family and community encouragement. This then is the kind of intriguing picture which can be built up through statistical investigation and interpretative understanding of the role of cultural family and community issues.

However, there are some intriguing puzzles when we begin to unpick the process of measurement in higher education. It is not our intention to summarize the results of the research in detail or to provide an explanatory treatment of the statistical techniques involved at this stage. Rather, it is our aim to explore some of the consequences of measuring educational phenomena and undertaking statistical treatments of the data obtained in research on higher education. This both reveals some important sequelae of higher education research and how we make sense of it. It also serves as preparation for subsequent treatments of evidence-based or evidence-informed practice and policy in the next chapter.

It is assumed that there are internal characteristics inside the students that are responsible for the overt manifestations of distress. Indeed, this discourse of interiority is a central plank in the kind of research, publication and practice that seeks to establish that care and personal development should be at the heart of new educational regimes. Wooton (2002: 354) puts it as follows:

> I have been deeply troubled by the lack of confidence and self-belief demonstrated by many of the young people in my charge, so much so that I am driven to determine why this should be. I had imagined, somewhat naïvely, that when I was to begin teaching higher education students some years ago I would find them highly motivated, eager to learn and challenge, keen to argue and debate. The reality was and still is that many of them are unsure of their own abilities, express feelings of inadequacy and find 'getting started' on assessment work an unbearably daunting prospect.

The interiority of the students' attitudinal and cognitive limitations mirrors the interiority of her own 'deeply troubled' state. This, however, is a usual though somewhat simplistic model of human communicative processes and social being, and seems to imply a curious nominalism, such that their self-directed attitude and cognition is seen as a precedent and cause of their actions. A further noteworthy aspect of this nominalism is the implied idea that the individual exists before society, and society was created subsequently as a result of a social contract between individuals. Alternatively, one could propose that 'limiting self-beliefs' and the like might well reflect a realistic appraisal of the limitations upon one's material powers at one's particular place in the world and might not be so readily adjusted through counselling or motivational interviewing. Indeed, the 'life of the mind', for all we know, may well always have been a minority interest in the world's major civilisations. Nevertheless, despite these provisos, there remains a strong conviction that there is something inside. More to the point, there are things in there that we can measure.

Measuring internal psychological characteristics, of course, is far from easy. We might be after cognitive or attitudinal measures, or even 'knowledge' or skill itself. As Preece (2002) reminds us, there are many assumptions involved in the statistical procedures that are often employed in research in education. One needs to be able to measure things in such a way that the values have certain properties. To illustrate this, let us go back to Steven's (1951) four-part typology of data, where measurements may have properties that allow them to be classified as nominal, ordinal, interval or ratio. Most of the statistical procedures employed demand data of at least interval level – where we can be sure that all the intervals of our scale are of the same size – or preferably ratio level, such that we can meaningfully make sense of matters such as shared variance in correlation and regression or significant difference between different groups. Some optimists such as Labowitz (1967, 1970) have argued that the statistical tests are robust in the face of violations of their assumptions. There are others, such as Preece (2002), who insist on a variety of operations on the measurement process itself to ensure the additivity assumption of ratio data is sustainable. What is interesting about this entire discussion is that it is usually conducted about data and does not generally explore whether psychological characteristics, especially those measured with self-report questionnaires, can be meaningfully understood in this way. While it is not unreasonable to suppose that two people may differ in terms of how favourably they view their degree course, it may be somewhat fatuous to say (or imply) that one's attitude is twice as favourable as the others. This would need to be true in order to satisfy the ratio assumption, yet it seems difficult to sustain.

Nevertheless, researchers have approached the subject of study in higher education in the hope of discovering and measuring the internal characteristics of research participants, and many different kinds of self-report questionnaire have been devised to address this. Attempts have been made to measure individuals' motives and approaches to study. For example, Biggs' (1987) Study Processes Questionnaire (SPQ) explores motives and strategies – 'surface versus deep' approaches – used in learning. Using this kind of measure of depth of processing – a problematic notion, as we have argued earlier – Marton and Saljo (1984) discovered that students who adopted a 'deep' approach, seeking the meaning of material, appeared to understand material better than those adopting a 'surface' approach by memorizing information. Subsequently, Pintich and Degroot (1990) developed a measure called the Motivated Strategies for Learning Questionnaire, which intended to identify factors that could improve teaching and learning.

This research has an intuitive appeal, yet results suggest that students' self-reported approaches to studying do not correlate well with academic performance (Provost and Bond 1997). Provost and Bond (1997) themselves suggested that this is because these questionnaire measures or 'instruments' tend to address what students 'intend to do', rather than what they 'actually do', in order to learn material. Nevertheless, this has not particularly dampened spirits in the field, and questionnaire measures of study patterns, habits and attitudes are still widely deployed in research and guidance.

Even with measures that might be expected to correspond to students' performance in formal assessments, which count towards their degree, the results are often not encouraging. Nuhfer and Knipp (2006) report that a survey of students' knowledge did not correlate strongly with the results from a formal assessment in a course in the biological sciences. In the face of this diversity among measures, they directed their attention instead to the internal reliability of the questionnaire used in the knowledge survey. Rather than focus on the relationship of their measures to some sort of criterion, such as student success on the course, researchers often preoccupy themselves with the internal psychometric properties of the measures themselves.

A similar state of play exists when we consider the question of goals and motivation. Here, the situation is more propitious because there are some established relationships between motivation performance and a success situation. For example, the literature consistently indicates that setting specific and challenging goals results in improvements in performance compared to the results obtained when participants have less well-articulated goals such as 'do your best' (Mento *et al.* 1987, Locke and Latham 1990, Locke 1996). There is a track record of research attempting to apply goal-setting strategies in education (e.g. Wentzel 1991, Gillat and Sulzer-Azaroff 1994, Berry 1996), but White (2002) identifies that this has yet to be fully exploited in the study of university students. Once again, the measurement of the property with a self-report questionnaire is expounded. The possibilities for developing this further as an end in itself are anticipated. As White (2002: 298) says:

> Once acceptable levels of reliability and validity are achieved, the Student Goals and Behaviour Questionnaire can be used to assess student attitudes and behaviour to goal-setting, identify problem areas in student goal-setting, and implement changes to the curriculum where students are taught to set specific high goals.

The decision that goal-setting as a part of the curriculum in higher education is a good idea has more or less already been taken and the author is enthusiastically unfurling a programme of research to refine the questionnaire, or 'instrument' as it are often called.

This is not to say that these properties of people, such as orientations to study and motivation, are capriciously invented by researchers. Far from it; they are assiduously anchored to data which is consensually taken as evidence of their existence. Rather, the interesting thing is that once they are understood in these terms they take on a life of their own and generate yet more research.

The cognitive activities which we imagine underlie university study and students' subjective experience of study are opened up and shaped by these new technologies that extend our gaze into the human psyche. Once they have been established, like the philosopher Hacking describes in his work on the 'looping effect of human kinds', they represent a way in which people can make sense of themselves and others. Moreover, 'the looping effect' describes the way in which, in human studies, the understanding can affect the people who are understood in this way. The looping effect, says Hacking, 'is about how a causal understanding, if known by those who are understood, can change their character, can change the kind of person that they are. This can lead to a change in the causal understanding itself' (Hacking 1995: 351). The identification of kinds of people, or properties of people, and their measurement is bound up with other kinds of administrative or governmental activities. Hacking writes: 'The search for human kinds that conform to psychological or social laws is inextricably intertwined with prediction and reform' (Hacking 1995: 360). This is particularly true in a society like ours that seeks to manage the experience of learning and extend it through strata of the population who have hitherto escaped its grasp. The measure of orientation to learning, knowledge and motivation unfold as a kind of toolkit to facilitate this process.

Conclusion: The assumptions of human enquiry

In conclusion, let us sum up some of the themes in this chapter concerned with how we might know about educational processes in college or university life. We have drawn upon examples such as phenomenography, the role of gender in higher education studies and the measurement of cognitive, attitudinal and motivational characteristics and discussed what this might mean.

Phenomenography and reflective practice have brought the processes of teaching, learning and personal development into view, yet at the same time they are reminiscent of the process described by Foucault under the heading of 'the care of the self', that is that they help to constitute and name the phenomena they are exploring, and involve judgements concerning appropriate and inappropriate ways to understand and develop ideas about the objects of enquiry. The availability of these methods, then, means that we should be particularly vigilant as to the political and ethical agendas which they bring with them.

Constructs drawn from other areas of social enquiry, such as gender studies, might, once they are imported into educational enquiry, tempt us to accept a somewhat rigid formulation of how people make sense of their phenomenal worlds, so that the resulting understandings of gender may look more like popular self-help literature than a more nuanced inquiry. Moreover, they sometimes leave unexamined important questions about autonomy, agency and creativity, and do not grasp the sheer flexibility that human beings bring to the educational encounter.

This sense of stasis in the student response to educational experiences is also to be found in the attempts that we have described to measure the educationally relevant psychometric properties of students. If students are formulated, measured and defined in terms of their orientations to study and their motivations for attending university, then this brings with it the kinds of consequences which Hacking (1995) identifies as the looping effect of human kinds. The dimensions identified by researchers take on a curious reality all of their own, and become part of – or at least reinforce – the repertoire of ways in which people themselves see their psychological interior. Moreover, this becomes part of the way in which the curious reader, anxious to understand the process of student learning, comes to conceptualize the *modus operandi* and performance of academic work.

5

Evidence-based practice in higher education

> Could quantification settle important issues of public policy? Experience was often disappointing, but hope sprang eternal.
> (Porter 1995: 152)

Introduction: The drive for evidence

This chapter explores the different approaches that have been taken to the role of evidence-based practice in education. In Chapter 1 we introduced some of the issues surrounding evidence-based or evidence-informed practice in the educational field and indicated that a good deal of the inspiration for this comes from the healthcare arena. As Clegg (2005) documents, in the UK the political factors informing the debates about evidence-based practice take their cue from the enthusiasm of New Labour policy-makers in the 1990s and early twenty-first century. David Blunkett, when he was Minister for Education, said in 2000 that 'we need social scientists to help determine what worked and why, and what types of policy initiative are likely to be most effective' (in Evans and Benefield 2001: 527). This impetus to establish efficiency and effectiveness in public policy was linked to funding initiatives and the imperative to ensure demonstrable value for money by means of improvements in measurable outcomes. The discourse of 'what works' has, therefore, become important in determining the value of research outputs. Educational research has regularly been criticized for failing to deliver proper cumulative evidence that could inform policy and practice and, in contradiction to this, being insufficiently responsive to policy-makers' needs for information.

At the start of the twenty-first century, David Blunkett summed up the UK Government's determination to drive the agenda towards more extensive and effective use of research evidence. As Clegg (2005) notes, a good deal of infrastructure is in place to encourage this. The close relationship of the evidence-based movement to clinical research in health is readily apparent from the agendas of many of the organizations involved in this infrastructure. The Evidence for Policy and Practice Information and Co-ordinating Centre (2006), part of the Social Science Research Unit at the Institute of Education in London, was established in 1993. The Centre's aims are closely aligned to those of the Cochrane Collaboration (2007) set up in 1993 as an international organization involved with the preparation of systematic reviews. In addition, the NHS-based Centre for Reviews and Dissemination (2007) was established in January 1994, and is closely allied with the National Institute for Clinical Excellence (2007). These initiatives are organized around the core notion that research should inform policy and practice and that appropriate and useful evidence can be sifted and condensed through systematic review (Torgerson 2003, Clegg 2005).

The species of educational research that have often been seen as most valuable have been quantitative in nature and have involved comparisons – either natural or specially contrived experiments. While these experimental methods have been accelerating the productivity of chemists, physicists and biologists since the nineteenth century, educators and educational researchers have only recently tried to make education an experimental discipline. Experiments are often done in an atmosphere of controversy, so it is usual to find them being subject to criticism, re-evaluation and attempts at replication. Rather than putting a stop to controversy in educational studies then, evidence-based approaches are often the very things that spark it off and sustain it.

This process of attempting to make education a research-led, experiment-based discipline has been enthusiastically pursued in the US, too. Echoing Blunkett's call in the UK, US representative Michael Castle claimed:

> Education research is broken in our country . . . and Congress must work to make it more useful . . . Research needs to be conducted on a more scientific basis. Educators and policy-makers need objective, reliable research.
>
> (Michael Castle, US Representative, in National Research Council 2002: 28)

It is appealing to think of basing practice on the most up-to-date, valid and reliable research findings but, at the same time, practitioners rarely alter their practice on the basis of research results (Birnbaum 2000, Trinder 2000). Indeed, there is some evidence that whilst practitioners adhere to the position that evidence-based practice is a good idea, they are equally adroit at accounting for the fact that they do not use it – for example the difficulty of library access or the lack of time (Crawford *et al.* 2002).

However, there are some trends in the evidence-based practice movement that indicate a rather different agenda. What is less often remarked upon in discussions of the subject is that the 'evidence-based' or 'accountability' movement facilitates governmental incursion into educational research and practice so as to subject them to governmental regulation. In North America, federal policy research in education has come increasingly to value randomized controlled trials or randomized field trials as the 'gold standard' in the evidence-based movements that have appealed so highly to policy-makers and senior public administrators at the federal level (Tierney 2001, Cochran-Smith 2002, Lather 2004a).

Evidence-based approaches dominated by experimental methods are often advocated as a debunking mechanism, where scientifically oriented researchers seek to undermine the claims of other practitioners whose methods they see to be outmoded, harmful or lacking in evidential support.

On both sides of the Atlantic, as Lather (2004a) notes, science, money and politics have combined with pre-positioned capability and sweetheart contracts awarded to self-identified 'ambitious researchers' (Burtless 2002: 193) to consolidate a governmental role in the definition and adoption of 'one-best way' in scientific educational research. For example, this agenda was purveyed most strenuously in a volume published in 2002 called *Evidence matters: Randomized trials in education research* (Boruch and Mosteller 2002). Mosteller, then Professor Emeritus of mathematics at Harvard University, was well known from his work in the 1970s as an architect of 'gold standard' randomized controlled clinical trials in healthcare research. In their introduction, the co-editors express agreement with the US government's interest in research 'quality' in educational enquiry. Boruch *et al.*'s text is rife with phrases such as 'standards of evidence' and 'scientific rigor'. In the interests of inclusiveness, 'other kinds of research' can be employed as 'augmentation' to controlled studies, provided 'scientific standards' can be delineated and not compromised. Boruch and Mosteller (2002: 2) 'worry about ideology parading as intellectual inquiry', so their task is to persuade sponsoring agencies 'that there is no easier way to get the answers to the right question' (2002: 3) than randomized field trials. Dismayed by the paucity of 'good studies' (2002: 4), they call for political and administrative support for 'rigorous research' to remedy the bad reputation of educational enquiry so far.

At the same time, the governmental agenda does not always roll forwards like a well-oiled juggernaut. Sometimes policy-makers themselves appear impatient of the painstaking process of stitching together evidence and policy. The idea of policy being 'evidence-based', gained a particularly high profile in government circles in June 2005 when Louise Casey, at the time the director of the government's anti-social behaviour unit, was alleged to have initially remarked that 'doing things sober is no way to get things done' while addressing a conference organized by the Home Office and Association of Chief Police Officers. She was then reported to have gone on to say that: 'there is an obsession with evidence-based policy. If Number 10 says bloody evidence-based policy one more time, I'll deck them one . . .' (Johnston 2005). The reaction from the nation's press to these comments ranged from angry demands for Ms Casey's resignation to hilarity. However, there are indications that in some quarters there are people who share Ms Casey's disdain for 'evidence-based' policy and practice. More subtly, as Lather (2004b) notes, the evidence-based movement intervenes in the educational arena in a way that is hard to separate from the socially conservative, neo-liberal agenda that can be seen at work on the politics of many developed nations. In addition, this kind of 'activist interventionism and expansion of the scope of government' (Shaker 2002) contrasts oddly with the rhetoric of choice, empowerment and liberation from 'one size fits all' state provision and control which is foregrounded in contemporary political rhetoric. A legislative agenda concerning the scientificity of study design is pervasive in both the US and UK.

Within this framework, objectivity is enshrined, and prediction, explanation and verification are prioritized over description, interpretation and discovery. An epistemological sovereignty is evoked in the US National Research Council (2002) report where, despite acknowledgement of the varieties of research available, the authors consistently return to delineating and applying the principles of 'high-quality science' (Shavelson *et al.* 2003). Indeed, features that more progressive researchers build in to the research process – including the specificities of values and politics, human volition and program variability, cultural diversity, multiple disciplinary perspectives, factors related to partnerships with practitioners, the ethical considerations of randomized controlled designs – are seen as getting in the way of an engineering approach to educational science (Lather 2004b). There is, behind all this, a unified theory of scientific advancement with its expectation that a unified method will be applicable across the physical, life and social sciences. This is yoked to a model of efficiency whereby the least money should be spent to achieve the desired effect. In this context, slogans like 'scientifically sound' and 'politically objective' represent a beacon of hope against officially sanctioned disdain for the diversification of research styles and paradigms in educational enquiry. The widespread 'discontent with the state of current knowledge of what works in education' (Cook and Payne 2002: 150) has, apparently, resulted from the 'rejection of experimental design'. This itself was identified by Cook and Payne (2002: 151) as 'probably a major cause of the impoverished current state of knowledge' and they specifically blame qualitative researchers such as Eisner, Guba, Lincoln, Patton, Stake and Stufflebeam.

The UK situation: The Higher Education Academy and the search for evidence

At a professional level, the UK's approach to evidence-based policy and practice in higher education has been a little more demure. The aggressive promotion of an experimental, randomized, controlled trial methodology has been less apparent. In 2004, the UK's Higher Education Academy held a symposium entitled: 'The meaning of evidence-based practice in higher education: How far can we take it?', which reflected a high level of interest in evidence-based approaches to teaching and external examining in UK higher education. Subsequently, the Higher Education Academy stated its commitment to, for example, providing the higher education sector with a firm evidence base to inform the widening participation agenda. Jackson's (2004) Working Paper to inform and stimulate discussion at the higher education symposium considered the extent to which practice could be evidence-based or supported by evidence; the different purposes for which evidence may be used; whether all or best available evidence is used; whether evidence is used selectively or deceptively; and whether a practice is evidence-based or evidence-informed.

This catalogue of considerations is however, like the US variants, firmly embedded within a notion of scientificity that foregrounds considerations of 'objectivity' and 'bias', as if there were a single, unequivocal way to handle nature and make sense of evidence. For example, Jackson proposed a 'continuum of intentionality' to illustrate how approaches might vary from the 'completely biased', where the decision is made and evidence is found to support it, to the other end where the approach is 'balanced' or 'objective'. There is an assumption that the evidence itself will somehow be beyond the value judgements, worldviews and presuppositions of the people making decisions. Those who are willing to learn that their propositions are not sound, yet who are prevented by their subconscious perceptual biases from undertaking 'truly balanced' enquiry, are positioned in the middle of the continuum.

Thus, like their US counterparts, UK practitioners and scholars have frequently made use of the kind of fact-value distinction popularized in the social sciences by Quetelet and Comte in the nineteenth century. This position assumes the inherent neutrality and separation from human agency of the evidence. However, a great many sociological and psychological descriptions of social phenomena are 'integrally evaluative' (Davydova and Sharrock 2003). Moreover, a number of thinkers have, since the mid-twentieth century, problematized the idea of factual descriptions of social life. Winch (1958) Louch (1967) and Searle (1969) have put forward the view that all observations of the social world, as far as they produce meaningful descriptions, involve a strong element of evaluation.

However, in the Higher Education Academy's deliberations there is an ongoing faith that somehow the confusion and ambiguity which they identify merely overlays a more solid layer of evidence that the clear-sighted scholar can appreciate. The problems with using evidence were formulated as being to do with the way we use evidence reflecting 'our own natural biases' and our tendencies to interpret and use evidence in ways consistent with our beliefs and understandings of the world. People may be less inclined to, or may be resistant to, accept evidence inconsistent with our worldviews. Furthermore, the organizational, political, operational and complex social worlds in which we live may constrain our ability to absorb and make 'objective sense' of evidence. We therefore have to move from the idealistic world of 'evidence use' into the more realistic world of complexity thinking (Stacey 2000). Thus the worlds of objectivity (rational, scientific, commonsense ways of thinking and behaving) and subjectivity (seemingly illogical thinking and behaviours) intertwine. Jackson (2004) maintained that a continuum of intentionality is necessary for operating in a complex world. Thus there is a lingering hope that somehow the ambiguity, contestation and bias can be top-sliced off to leave a solid core of factuality which would presumably be useful in improving the UK's higher education situation. There is also an assumption in much of this thinking, as Clegg (2005: 424) observes, that the relationship between evidence and practice is a one-way street, with results flowing from evidence to practice and that it is somehow possible to have evidence that is ontologically prior to practice. This might be sustainable in medicine, where laboratory work can inform practice, but this separation is far less likely to obtain in education.

In similar vein, Coe and Fitz-Gibbon (2004) observed that the interpretation of evidence is context dependent; it is often incomplete or equivocal; it may be complex, difficult to interpret or open to more than one interpretation. Knight (2004) noted that where evidence is available it may not be fit for purpose; it is frequently hard to interpret – forming interpretations is easy but Knight claims it is not always easy to form 'well-grounded interpretations'. In Coe and Fitz-Gibbon's view, the evidence for many questions is elusive and intractable; getting sufficient information is often expensive, slow and difficult. Moreover, evidence is complicated so it therefore needs to be mediated and is often incomplete so it needs to be complemented. The perspicacious scholar will need to 'champion' evidence, or even strong forms of it will be ignored. It was also noted that a changing and diverse environment means that there are inherent limitations to evidence as a basis for making future predictions.

Jackson (2004) includes a discussion of the 'diversity and richness of evidence'. He concludes that in higher education decision making there is a need for both descriptive, contextual, incidental evidence and factual, objective, analytical, synthetic evidence. McBride and Schostak (1995) recognized a whole variety of sources of data that could constitute evidence, such as student work, registers, student records, lesson plans, institutional brochures, policy statements, photographs, and video/audio and self-report diaries. From a business point of view, evidence could constitute memos, minutes of meetings, project plans, budgets, specifications of roles and relationships or mission statements. Clegg *et al.* (2004) described a range of evidence including interview data from student focus groups, teachers, lecturers, policy-makers, staff and educational developers; surveys of current practice; reports of external examiners and external peer reviewers; and survey questionnaires. Other suggested forms of evidence that may be suitable include email conversations, practice case studies (Nicol and MacFarlane-Dick 2004), evaluation of practice studies (Jackson *et al.* 2004), scientific research and syntheses of the findings of the research (Gough 2004, Jackson *et al.* 2004, Leask and White 2004, Nicol and MacFarlane-Dick 2004). It was suggested that effective evidence about successful practice often appeared to be of the 'conversational' type – such as might be derived from narrative, vignettes of practice, 'warts and all' depictions, and 'messy' case studies. Jackson acknowledges that any area of professional practice in higher education will have its own body of evidence to draw upon and its own practices to create and use evidence.

Jackson (2004) notes that evidence-based decision making (EBDM) and evidence-based practice in medicine (EBPM) focuses on the practitioner finding and critically appraising the relevance of best research evidence to satisfy a particular enquiry. If the evidence is judged to be relevant, the knowledge is acted upon. Jackson (2004) quotes Morris (2004), who translated a definition for evidence-based medicine (EBM) into the field of teaching:

> Evidence-based teaching is the conscientious, explicit and judicious use of current best evidence in making decisions about the teaching and learning experience offered to students. The practice of evidence-based teaching means integrating individual academic and pedagogic expertise with the best available external evidence from systematic research.

In Chapter 1 we presented the outline of evidence-based practice in healthcare and the way it has been imported into the educational field. However, there are some important differences. Hammersley (2000: 163) notes that, in medicine, the major focus has been on the quality of healthcare practice, whereas in education, much of the debate has focused on the quality of research. Despite claims to the effect that evidence-based practice is a 'radically new venture' (Hammersley 2000: 164), research-based teaching has a considerable pedigree and educators have for a long time been aware of its limitations. The renewed emphasis on experimental designs yielding quantitative data as a source of evidence bespeaks a curious amnesia about the history of educational research itself. The enthusiasm for qualitative methodology in educational enquiry from the 1970s to the 1990s emerged from increasing dissatisfaction and difficulty in measuring what is educationally significant, and with the limitations of the causal models popular at the time, given the acknowledged importance of 'interaction effects'. Consequently, says Hammersley, educational researchers were at the forefront of 'philosophical and methodological disputes' (Hammersley 2000: 167) concerning the process of human enquiry that are still unresolved to this day. For example, the replicability of a piece of research does not necessarily clarify matters due to the 'complex web of relationships' (Hammersley 2000: 168) found in many naturalistic settings which make it difficult to resolve any causal relationships decisively.

Thus, the extent to which the kinds of problems that educators confront are susceptible to solution by research is precisely the question. 'The importance of contextual judgment mandates a great caution in adapting the medical model. Formulas for transparent accountability are more about politics than about quality of service' (Lather 2004b: 20).

The translation of the medical model of evidence-based practice into the educational arena is also problematic because even in medicine people do not necessarily adhere to its precepts. It is relatively rare to find practitioners who spend substantial portions of their time reading original research. General practitioners tend not to conduct their own information searches, but rely for their information on information brokers such as National Institute of Clinical Excellence guidelines. In this spirit, the Higher Education Academy is building databases to support a number of educational activities, such as an evidence-based approach in the field of personal development planning (Jackson *et al.* 2004).

Support for evidence-based practice in the UK Higher Education Academy is tempered with scepticism however. Jackson (2004) questions how well the evidence-based medicine practice model is actually understood. Within the UK higher education field there is a strong current of belief suggesting that randomized controlled trials as used in medicine and the synthesizing of evidence from such trials as a means of identifying best evidence for practice is inappropriate for higher education. The outcomes of research syntheses are also criticised, the lessons being difficult to imagine in practice. It is noted that ideas of policy or practice importation and 'best practice' involve naïve assumptions about the inherent genericism in often highly situated successes. It is also suggested that evidence-based practice becomes an ideology. With regard to policy, it is stressed that there is a need to find a way of understanding the evidence to inform policy development without believing that evidence, which is always limited in various ways, demonstrates, or justifies, the necessity to make a single policy option compulsory for all.

Despite the difficulties with evidence-based practice as a concept and the practical problems with its implementation in educational contexts, there remains considerable hope for its future. Paul Ramsden (2004), the chief executive of the Higher Education Academy, set out a vision of what the organization should achieve in promoting evidence-based practice in teaching and learning:

> We will ensure that the Academy sets an example that other countries will find hard to match when it comes to applying a professional, evidence-based approach to improving students' experiences throughout the UK . . . it will mean establishing a solid, easily accessible evidence base that will enable all staff who teach and support students' learning to choose the course of action that will best achieve their goals.

The process of making sense of evidence: Models of science and models of practitioners

The process of drawing inferences from studies of educational processes is 'not only a question of statistical generalization, but must include a jump from the world of experience into the world of reason, assessment and theoretical judgment' (Holmberg *et al.* 1999: 160). In addition, it may be difficult for educators and researchers to fully grasp what a learning task means to the student. Evidence of the significance of learning experiences and educational interventions from the student's perspective is far less clearly defined in the research literature.

Bleakley (2005) describes the ways in which narrative and storytelling can add to the more conventionally rigorous inquiries favoured within evidence-based practice. As he remarks, qualitative studies have often been seen as 'soft', in contrast to the 'hard' sciences. Indeed, as Gherardi and Turner (2002) put it 'real men don't collect soft data'. Lather (2004a), in somewhat whimsical fashion, pursues these metaphors of 'hard' and 'soft' data into French feminist theory where Irigaray (1985) used psychoanalytically based arguments to pick apart the gender assumptions haunting the warp and weft of social science theory. Irigaray and Lather are concerned that we have naturalized masculinized language and logic to such an extent that we do not see the practical aspects of such domination. For example, we usually talk about 'hard' and 'soft' data rather than 'wet' and 'dry' data. Powerful epistemological regimes and systems of philosophy are designed to 'penetrate', interventions are 'engineered', 'we encourage one another to be "hard" on issues' (Olkowski 2000: 92). By contrast, at the less valued pole of research and theory, we have what has been described as the 'embarrassing emotion-fest' of women's work (Olkowski 2000: 93), interpreted as 'excess . . . wild or crazy, bizarre, remote, or meaningless' to the serious agendas of social policy (2000: 93). To be considered intelligible or useful, language has to conform to rigid hegemonic systems of formulation and standards of truth which cleave to a logic of solid mechanics (Lather 2004a: 766). What Irigaray calls 'fluid economies . . . make us shudder' within the 'order of good sense' (Irigaray 1985: 99).

To borrow from Foucault's work, it seems that naming, classifying and analyzing the components of educative practice so as to determine what works most cost-effectively, all helps to work toward disciplining people through normalizing. Practitioners and educators come to evaluate and monitor themselves as they work. Reflective practice, the proliferation of specifications for good teaching and learning, and cost-effectiveness considerations mean that those who work in universities are enjoined to constantly scrutinize themselves. Such governmentality is 'as much about what we do to ourselves as what is done to us' (Danaher *et al.* 2000: 83).

As scholars have struggled to make sense of the attempts at government regulation of education research in the US, a number of them (e.g. Lather 2004a, 2004b) have turned to a further insight from Foucault, to the effect that the privileged position accorded to the experimental, scientific approach to evidence-based practice has not occurred entirely for scientific reasons. The experimental, randomized controlled trial approach has, in all likelihood, been adopted as much for political reasons as epistemological ones. As Foucault has it, the 'privilege accorded to . . . "the sciences of man" is based on the "political arithmetic"' (Foucault 1998: 323) that makes particular kinds of discourse both possible and necessary. Claims to scientificity are discursive events. Here the 'inexact knowledges' become 'a field of strategic possibilities' (Foucault 1998: 320).

In Trinder's (2000) review of evidence-based practice across a range of public services in the UK, she makes sense of its appeal and rapid influence in terms of the need in 'post-traditional societies' for ways of managing risk in the face of suspicion of experts and professionals. At the same time, paradoxically, in detraditionalized societies, there is a degree of dependence on experts as never before. If we add to this context the push toward value-for-money, the ascendancy of managerialism, consumerism, and the growing prominence of political discourses emphasizing accountability and performance, then it appears that public services are more or less primed for an evidence-based transformation. In the neo-liberal political framework that prevails in many developed nations, there is a strong suggestion that neutrality can be established through protocol and procedure, and such practices are apt to prevail in an 'explosion of auditable management control systems' (Trinder 2000: 9). This is a solution to the problem of managing 'quality' issues through the promised effectiveness of producing and applying evidence, which sidesteps the troublesome issue of professional judgement and the political problem of having powerful professionals.

Although 'a product of its time' (Trinder 2000: 5), the problem remains that little evidence is available that suggests that evidence-based practice actually works (2000: 2).

In a sense, evidence-based practice is not so much about designing educational interventions as designing practitioners. The problems with translating the model from healthcare to education and the difficulties of relating the outcomes of educational research to educational practice, have been rehearsed above and the difficulties have been expounded by many authors. On the other hand, the spectre of evidence-based practice makes the educator or practitioner into a different kind of being. Instead of someone who can rely on their expertise and knowledge to work effectively with students, we have instead a reflexive self, or reflexive practitioner, constantly wondering whether what they are doing is good enough. In this sense it fits in with the developments we have already mentioned, where 'reflexive selves' from Giddens's work and 'reflexive practitioners' from Schön's, are already hard at work crafting their identities. There is a pervasive sense that one should always be looking for evidence that one's educational work is effective. Spare moments spent harvesting articles from the proliferation of journals dealing with higher education topics, reading through the Higher Education Academy's summaries for 'busy academics' and a relentless self-examination are all part of this new form of consciousness that is being cultivated. We are not suggesting that this is a literal description of the state of mind of every educator in the post-compulsory education sector. Rather, it is as Foucault would have it, a matter of the 'technologies of the self':

> technologies of the self, which permit individuals to effect by their own means or with the help of others . . . operations on their own bodies and souls, thoughts, conduct, and way of being, so as to transform themselves in order to attain a certain state of happiness, purity, wisdom, perfection, or immortality. (Foucault 1988: 16)

In this framework, evidence-based practice, or evidence-informed practice, is a profoundly ethical approach because, for Foucault, the term 'ethics' designates the arena in which individuals act upon themselves in order to become 'moral subjects of [their] own actions' (Davidson 1994: 118). Through this process, people come to govern their own thoughts and actions. The ethical government of the self in this way was divided by Foucault into four segments, comprising *ontology*, *ascetics*, *deontology* and *telos* (Foucault 1984). In this way, the educator under an evidence-based practice regime becomes an ethical agent through the technologies of the self whereby they come to govern their conduct.

Ontology refers to the ethical substance, or part of the person or his or her behaviour concerned with moral conduct. For example, in planning and preparing for a teaching and learning event, the ethical substance on which the educator works includes their behaviour as an educator and this also infuses the physical materials and teaching aids that they produce. In order to act on themselves and their behaviour as an ethical substance, educators undertake an array of self-forming activities, or *ascetics*, through which they can change themselves in the direction of becoming an evidence-informed, reflexive practitioner. These activities might include consultation with colleagues or mentors, participation in training programmes and sifting through evidence relating to effective teaching practice in order to develop strategies for maximizing the potential learning gain for students. The third aspect to this ethical process of government of the self is *deontology*, which relates to the mode of subjection, in the sense of who we are when we submit ourselves to governance in this manner. In engaging in evidence-informed learning-maximization and risk-minimization strategies, an educator's mode of subjection is as a person who might potentially fail to facilitate the occurrence of learning, who might cause offence, who might cause harm to students through practices which are exclusionary or discriminatory, and so on. Finally, *telos* is 'the kind of being to which we aspire when we behave in a moral way' (Foucault 1984: 355). In this instance, the kind of being to which we might aspire as evidence-informed educators through the governance of self was as a 'good' or 'effective' teacher, adding value to the students in their care.

Although this account could be thought of as slightly exaggerated, it is our purpose here to bring home the point that while evidence itself might be ambiguous, and it may not be of the kind that policy-makers desperately want, the evidence-based movement is cultivating a particular kind of self-regard on the part of teaching staff.

This mode of being relates also to the reflective practice that is encouraged among the participants on courses intended to develop teaching skills. The reflexivity and self-scrutiny demanded of reflexive pratitioners is usually shared with others, in training courses, in workshops, through the process of mentorship and appraisal. This is reminiscent of what Foucault had to say about how the process of confession has shaped the modern, Western concept of the subject – the self or the person. Foucault talked about how confessions are demanded of us by a range of professional and regulatory groups such as doctors, government officials, judges, teachers or parents. In the light of modern psychiatry, therapy and educational practice, we tend to see such contemporary variants of confession as liberating, as therapeutic, as lifting a weight off our shoulders or as enabling professional development. Foucault suggests that confessions are not inherently liberating, but that we have been encouraged to see them that way by the very powers that extract confessions from us. Because so many different groups demand confessions 'for your own good', or to bring us into a spiritual or personal state of grace, we automatically see confession as something good. A reading of Foucault implies that the idea of confession as part of a therapeutic process or as part of a kind of professional development is not somehow unproblematically true, it is instead a part of our culture and an effect of power.

But the 'I' that we speak about is no longer an obvious and transparent thing. It needs exposing through diligent self-examination, a mystery even to myself, something I must dig into my own consciousness to discover:

> . . . the particular type of discourse and particular techniques which supposedly reveal our deepest selves . . . in confession after confession to oneself and to others, this *mise en discourse* has placed the individual in a network of relations of power with those who

> claim to be able to extract the truth of these confessions through their possession of the keys of interpretations.
>
> (Dreyfus and Rabinow 1982: 174)

Or as Rose puts it:

> The individual was to be taught to control his own life . . . This entailed a training in the minute arts of self-scrutiny, self-evaluation, and self-regulation ranging from the control of the body, speech and movement in school . . . to the Puritan practices of self-inspection and obedience to divine reason. (Rose 1990: 113)

Confession in this sense is a type of reflexive hermeneutics. It is a sort of self-discovery which is at the same time self-creating. The reflexive, evidence-informed educator is a monumental achievement, and one which has only a tenuous relationship to the weight of evidence itself.

At the same time, the work of Jackson and his colleagues and the more virulent activities of the enthusiasts for randomized controlled trials in the US, represents a project to redesign knowledge. Just as surely as the positivists of the nineteenth century who sought to eliminate normative or metaphysical aspects of knowledge, the contemporary enthusiasts for trials are redesigning knowledge toward a new aesthetic. The 'web-scrubbing' of US government-funded websites to eliminate material that is not germane to contemporary policy, the enthusiasm for experimental randomized controlled trials of educational interventions and the advocacy of 'systematic reviews' to synthesize 'high-quality' evidence all serve to builds a particular version of what really useful knowledge should look like.

Pillars of the UK social science community such as Ann Oakley are at pains to point out that 'evidence of effectiveness' is best provided through some form of comparative experimentation. She asks:

> Why did experimental methods appear only to belong to natural science and to doctors? Why did they not seem to be owned equally

> by social science and other groups of professionals – for example social workers, teachers and those involved in criminal justice and crime prevention? What was so special about those professions that made them immune to the need to show that their interventions in other people's lives worked and did more good than harm?
>
> (Oakley 2000: 19)

Moreover, in her recent book, Oakley comments that, in the context of evaluation, anything else but randomized, controlled trials 'is a "disservice to vulnerable people . . .' (Oakley 2000: 318).

These persuasive arguments show just how effective the discourse is. This is reminiscent of what Foucault (1972) wrote about in *The Archaeology of Knowledge.* Here he speaks of 'discursive positivities' that constitute the conditions under which something may *become* knowledge. In terms of Foucault's archaeological project, the discursive positivities are not systems of knowledge nor are they collections of bits of more or less true knowledge. Organized sciences such as the kind that are being established around educational enquiry are thus established on the basis of discursive positivities.

The repeated, enthusiastic urgings towards a particular model of science that we can see among those who promote the experimental approach to studies of education are in the process of putting knowledge through a number of stages identified by Foucault. In becoming a science, a discursive formation crosses a number of thresholds. First, comes the threshold of positivity, when the discursive formation is first put into operation. Second, the stage which we can see now is one of epistemologization, where a discipline – or powerful interests within it – start to dominate and systematically rearrange knowledge. Third, there is the stage of scientificity which formulates its own rules of articulation, which we can see in educational research when people write about the 'quality' of research and adjudicate between studies on the basis of how closely they resemble a randomized controlled trial. We can also see this in the epistemological stall set out by the UK's Higher Education Academy whose authors carve out a vision of evidence that is potentially separable from the 'bias' and 'interpretation' originating in the human agents around it. Finally, there is a stage of formalization, when a discipline fully formalizes its own principles, axioms and methods. Perhaps the progress of the new, policy-oriented, experimental model of educational research is reaching this stage.

This series of stages, however, does not obey strict chronological laws, nor does the sequence of 'thresholds' have to happen in this order. The key point here is that knowledge, as it is shaped and developed by human enquiry, takes its form as an effect of discourse. Thus, Foucault's view contrasts with many conventional histories of science where knowledge is what one ends up with as the ultimate aim of discourse. Instead, in this view, knowledge is a possible effect within the field of discourse – knowledge is 'that of which one can speak in a discursive practice.'

Whether evidence informs policy, of course, is another matter entirely. As Whitty reminds us politics itself is shaped by symbolic considerations that may have little to do with the policy's material effects, and the focus sometimes has to be on what can be done, instead of on what might really make a difference (Levin 2005: 23, Whitty 2006).

However, what we are seeing develop is a process whereby evidence-informed practice is extended as an aesthetic practice. It is about making everything look nice and tidy. The experimental research allows us to adjudicate between, say, different teaching methods or different widening-access strategies. Then the appropriate action can be taken by evidence-informed practitioners and policy-makers to ensure that the public money spent on education is expended most efficiently as a result of 'high-quality' research. The untidy situation delineated by researchers and practitioners who often cannot quite make the process look like this is granted far less credibility and can be allowed to disappear below the line of sight and vanish as government bodies and funding agencies revamp their websites.

Alternative formulations of evidential adequacy

This picture might appear somewhat bleak from the point of view of those who would like to pursue a more creative approach to the study of education. Therefore, to conclude this chapter, we will consider some possibilities for research and practice in higher education that might facilitate breaking away from the kinds of disciplinary constraints that we have identified earlier.

First of all, many philosophers and historians of science have identified that human enquiry is not always constrained by rule sets governing the quality of evidence. As Paul Feyerabend (1924–94) claimed in his book *Against Method*:

> There is not a single rule, however plausible, and however firmly grounded in epistemology, that is not violated at some time or other. It becomes evident that such violations are not accidental events, they are not results of insufficient knowledge or of inattention which might have been avoided. On the contrary, we see that they are necessary for progress. (Feyerabend 1975: 21)

In parallel with the hardening of scientific positions visible in the camp of the enthusiasts for experimental approaches to educational research, there is a different yet comparable tradition which has still not been entirely occluded. This tradition is devoted to establishing criteria which are rigorous, yet sufficiently generous to accommodate a broader range of inquiries into the educational enterprise. Guba and Lincoln (1989) unveiled some influential criteria whereby we can judge the value of interpretive research. Their criteria are applicable to a range of research in educational contexts, and were specifically developed to assist in programme evaluation. Thus they would be particularly apposite to the creative researcher or educator planning practice innovations. According to Guba and Lincoln:

> If we accept the definition of disciplined inquiry as set forth by Cronbach and Suppes (1969), it seems clear that standards for judging the quality of such inquiry are essential. The Cronbach and Suppes definition (1969: 15–16) suggests that disciplined inquiry 'has a texture that displays the raw materials entering into the arguments and the local processes by which they were compressed and rearranged to make the conclusions credible'. Thus a disciplined

> inquiry process must be publicly acceptable and open to judgements about the 'compression and rearrangement' processes involved. (1989: 228)

Guba *et al.*'s 'trustworthiness' criteria for research data include credibility, transferability, dependability and confirmability – which lie parallel to the traditional quantitative criteria of internal and external validity, reliability and objectivity, respectively. Subsumed within these were a number of methodological strategies for ensuring qualitative trustworthiness, such as audit trails; 'member checks' when coding, categorizing or confirming results with participants; peer debriefing; negative case analysis; structural corroboration; persistent observation; and referential material adequacy (Guba and Lincoln 1981, 1982, Lincoln and Guba 1985).

Of course, not everyone believes in an external reality independent of the process of enquiry, so even these criteria may be a little too restricting in that respect. If the research is being undertaken from a constructivist perspective, it is often predicated on the assumption that the realities which the researcher discovers are created in situ by the various actors involved; for example, by the people being observed and interrogated, the investigator and the wider community of readers and writers who see the finished product. Therefore, the question of credibility – or validity – needs some expansion, since if we were to take constructivism in a strong form we would believe that 'there is no ultimate benchmark to which one can turn for justification' (Lincoln and Guba 1985: 295), that is, there is no single reality that the researcher could hope to represent truthfully. However, even here the analysis and report are believed to need to 'ring true', or exhibit verisimilitude (Garman 1996: 19). Similarly, in relation to transferability, constructivist research usually aims to explore situated patterns within particular cases, rather than producing externally valid generalizations. Transferability to other contexts is then assessable by those who read the reported cases, provided they are given sufficiently detailed description and interpretation in the research accounts presented. In relation to confirmability, it is assumed that the value-free, objective enquirer is a myth, but that researchers should be reflexive and open about their positioning, and should be able to foreground personal and cultural values and the theoretical and epistemological stances from which the research is undertaken in a way that the reader can understand and take into account (Usher and Edwards 1994: 147–53). In this view, the research report should also present a construction grounded in the 'tangible realities' of the case, such as what was said, written or observed. Finally, in this perspective, it is recognized that literal replicability of findings is impossible, no matter what values and methods are deployed by the researchers. However, despite the expectation of near infinite variability, it is anticipated that amongst a particular community of researchers, if they perform an investigation among the same community of research participants at a similar time, then the 'data sets' obtained by these researchers, and thus their emergent understandings, will be largely comparable.

Guba and Lincoln's (1989) 'authenticity' criteria include: (i) fairness, as well as authenticity which may be; (ii) educative; (iii) ontological; (iv) catalytic; and (v) tactical. These are all recommended as means of evaluating the worth of research activity. Guba and Lincoln therefore go beyond attention just to the *methods* used in disciplined enquiry. Instead, they make ethical and relationship issues central to the process of inquiring into the lives of educators and learners. Premised upon the idea that research findings arise from the participants in the educational situation rather than from the researchers, fairness deals with the extent to which alternative constructions of the research process are explicitly made a part of the research. Educative authenticity 'represents the extent to which individual respondents' understanding of and appreciation for the constructions of *others* outside their stakeholding group are enhanced' (Guba and Lincoln 1989: 248). Ontological, catalytic and tactical authenticity relate respectively to research participants' ability to: (i) know and understand their own situation more deeply; (ii) be stimulated to *act* in order to improve their situation; and (iii) be *empowered* to act.

In this arena, where the research activity may involve creating stories around experiences, the nature of the narratives we create as practitioners and researchers are particularly crucial. Van

Maanen (1988) notes that if narrative forms of enquiry – specifically the 'impressionist tales' he advocates – are to be taken seriously, aesthetic and literary criteria become important:

> Literary standards are of more interest to the impressionist than scientific ones . . . In telling a tale, narrative rationality is of more concern than an argumentative kind. The audience cannot be concerned with the story's correctness, since they were not there and cannot know if it is correct. The standards are largely those of interest (does it attract?), coherence (does it hang together?), and fidelity (does it seem true?). Finally, since the standards are not disciplinary but literary ones, the main obligation of the impressionist is to keep the audience alert and interested. Unusual phrasings, fresh allusions, rich language, cognitive and emotional stimulation, puns and quick jolts to the imagination are all characteristic of the good tale. (Van Maanen 1988: 105–6)

In describing impressionist tales, particularly in the above excerpt, Van Maanen emphasizes the reliance on literary qualities over disciplinary ones. As has been have argued elsewhere (Dyson and Brown 2005) the idea of a research report derives from storytelling, statecraft and history in classical civilisations. In the present day, it has a peculiar status in that it must continually convince the reader that it is not 'merely' a piece of fiction. Without the impression of rigour attached to so-called 'solid' empirical research, accounts detailing interpretive enquiries will not be granted the status and authority associated with scientific scholarship. Making our work credible and believable has to do with how we tell the story. There is a rhetorical aspect to this storytelling such that the reader is steered towards the favoured interpretation and the research is designed and arguments are presented to support the favoured account of the findings. However, some would say that while it is *necessary* for narrative representations of research that the tales presented must engage readers and hold their attention, for the purposes of research it is not *sufficient*. Geelan (2001: 144) argues that research accounts must demonstrate: (i) that they are grounded in the researchers' personal experiences within educational settings; (ii) that the things they say are in some sense 'about' those experiences and about the educational establishment; and (iii) that the assertions and conjectures developed are significant and valuable within the field of education. Thus, Geelan is keen for us to consider that both the *verisimilitude* and the *utility* of the research for teachers and students become important criteria for its value.

Conclusion: Characterizing the relationship between research and practice

Research then is rather difficult to characterize. The version of enquiry promoted in policies designed to encourage evidence-based or evidence-informed practice is often an idealization, seldom achievable in practice. Very rarely do educational researchers have the opportunity or the resources to set up a randomized controlled trial of a particular programme or innovation. Often educational research takes place amongst the constant turbulence of innovation, quality assurance, confusion, reorganization and the experience of being asked to study things when they are already halfway over rather than at their inception. No wonder then that randomized controlled trials are so rare.

Yet this does not mean that educational research is well nigh impossible. It is hard to spend much time in the education system without becoming curious as to what goes on there. Education research emerges not from adherence to protocols demanding rigorous application of randomized controlled trials but from this curiosity. Even before research questions are formed so as to be empirically answerable, the imagination and curiosity of practitioners and researchers opens up new questions and novel ways of doing things, so that education is a constant process of 'research' by both the teacher and the students who have engaged themselves in the discipline.

The stimulation of this curiosity might go even further. It might yield the application of our combined critical intelligence to the idea of evidence-based practice itself. Some observers of communication in educational settings have tried to identify the mutual lines of influence between educator and student or between evidence and practice and to formulate new ways of addressing this complexity (Geelan 2003). This process may be seen as a dialectical one – that is one that moves to resolve contradictory ideas or arguments and brings into focus the full range of changes and interactions that occur in the world (Ollman 2003). In so doing, we might be advised to adopt an approach that proceeds from the whole to the part, from the social system inwards. The exchange of divergent ideas or arguments affords the identification and tracing of four kinds of relations: identity/difference, interpenetration of opposites, quantity/quality and contradiction. Rooted in this dialectical conception of reality, is the understanding that these relationships enable us to discover how something works or happened while simultaneously developing our understanding of the system in which such things could work or happen in just this way (Ollman 2003). That all sounds very abstract. In the next section then we shall take this dialectical approach a little further and describe some of the debates and critiques of evidence-based practice in healthcare a little more fully so as to show these dialectical processes at work.

Taking the idea of transformation and critique of evidence-based approaches a little further, we can identify a number of opposing positions that offer alternatives to a strong evidence-based approach. These often start from a position that is sceptical of the modernist conception of knowledge and the grand narrative of scientific progress with which it is often aligned. As Fox (2003) reminds us, many post-enlightenment theories of knowledge have an implicit agenda which assumes, in the manner of the popular 1990s science-fiction TV series *The X Files*, that 'the truth is out there'. They dress it up in various ways, for example in terms of concerns with validity and reliability, or perhaps in the case of qualitative research, in terms of authenticity or credibility. However, over the past few decades there have been many thinkers loosely clustering around postmodernist or post-structuralist viewpoints who have voiced an increasing suspicion of these kinds of 'grand narratives' or attempts to develop accounts of the 'truth' in a verifiable, finalized way. The concern with science, truth and rationality in modernism has been undermined by radical scepticism in postmodernism. The postmodern spirit then is one of suspicion of 'grand narratives' that purport to offer a unified or monolithic perspective on the world, what it means to be human or knowledge in general (Lyotard 1984). Derrida (1976) describes these kinds of narratives, for example philosophy, theology, science, biomedicine, or historical studies, as *logocentrisms*, whose objective is to achieve the *logos* – unmediated truth about the world. As Fox (2003) points out, there are many examples of apparently excellent science that have not yielded the hoped-for innovations in practice because researchers and practitioners hold different priorities and agendas. Furthermore, even in countries that nominally subscribe to similar scientific and pedagogic doctrines, practice can vary widely (Sweeney and Kernick 2002).

As a way of dealing with these kinds of phenomena, which would be problematic from the point of view of asserting a single right way of doing things, Fox proposes instead 'practice-based evidence', a different kind of relationship between research and practice. He advocates that, first, the pursuit of knowledge should be seen as a local and contingent process, rather than seeking grand generalizations. Second, he says that research activity should take a proactive stance towards differences and, rather than classify or place phenomena in a hierarchy, research should question whether certain forms of knowing are legitimated at the expense of knowledge as a whole. We should perhaps ask: whose interests does knowledge serve? Finally, says Fox, it would be desirable to see theory-building as an adjunct to practical activity, and evaluate it in terms of its ability to make a practical contribution to the setting where it originated. Together, these recommendations would help to dissolve the oppositions between the researcher and those being researched and the divide between research and practice. Fox desires to see ethically and politically engaged research that can contribute to practice-based evidence as well as evidence-based practice.

A further limitation on whether evidence-based practice can characterize what happens in educational encounters is to do with the nature of knowledge. The practical approach in a great deal of education still bears the imprint of 'see one, do one, teach one', as if knowledge could be acquired through observation and practice and then taught by the experienced practitioner to the novice. Yet there may be inherent restrictions on this process. According to Polanyi (1983) human knowing involves us knowing more than we can impart. A person might have comprehensive knowledge manifested through their ability to perform complicated actions, for example communicating flawlessly, yet at the same time they may be unable to explain their actions. The practical understanding identified here by Polanyi involves the ability to identify many small factors and to see how they fit together as a whole. In educational settings, if we follow Polanyi, we might identify an ongoing process of expert observation and skilful testing, which is often difficult to describe explicitly. To give an example of this, one of us (BB), early in his university teaching career developed a keen interest in the state of students' foreheads. If they looked as though they were becoming corrugated, it meant that further explanation was necessary.

If Polanyi is correct about this process of observation and testing, then this makes it difficult to itemize and characterize the kinds of skills that researchers or policy-makers are aiming to promote. Instead, they lie in those half-implicit areas of practice that we described as part of the *habitus* or *doxa* in Chapter 1.

Schön (1991) describes the competence of experienced practitioners to consider what they know intuitively in the midst of action as 'reflection-in-action'. Reflection-in-action is seen as a sort of unconscious and inarticulate 'conversation with the situation', where reframing and reworking of the problem leads to it being restructured and, hence, solved. The practitioner's absorption in the culture of the healthcare setting and their repertoire of examples, images, understandings and actions – rarely made explicit – enables a capacity for dealing with unique situations and individuals. This practical knowledge is gradually developed as the practitioner gains in experience (Dreyfus and Rabinow 1982). In educational work, tacit knowing concerning the nature of the problems encountered, and a tacit knowledge of the rules of the institutional and professional game – the *doxa* – constitute important parts of guessing what the students need and judgment of pedagogic conditions (Widdershoven-Heerding 1987). Experienced practitioners apply a range of experiential knowledge and strategies that are part of this *habitus*, in Bourdieu's sense of the term, which are hardly mentioned in the textbooks. Critical analysis of data is a key skill for students and practitioners to master, although there is evidence that the level of skill may be sub-optimal (Stern *et al.* 1995).

6

Conclusion: Philosophies of research and philosophies of higher education

In this conclusion we will revisit some of the themes with which we began this book, concerning the nature of research and the nature of the knowledge generating the post-compulsory education system and consider what we have learned about the process of coming to know about it.

We would like, first of all, to emphasize the importance of looking at context when considering pieces of research. Much of what we know comes not from a particular revolutionary finding alone, but because it forms part of a long tradition of enquiry. Experiments are believed to generate more credible results in part because of the traditions within which they are embedded. The legacy of positivism, the associations with the 'hard' sciences and the history of institutional support has made experiments bigger and more impressive, just as much as their elucidation of causal relationships. Thus, we would wish to re-emphasize the importance of looking at research results, methods and strategies in terms of their social context. Finally, we would like to give the reader some 'escape velocity' to begin exploring philosophical issues in educational enquiry themselves.

The purpose of research and the purpose of universities

Any consideration of the role of research and evidence-based practice in higher education is intimately bound up with what education is believed to be for. The purposes and ends we are trying to achieve will inform research agendas and methods chosen. In addition to the concerns we laid out in the first chapter concerning the nature and purposes of university life, it is worth re-emphasizing that there are a number of competing ideas and many turbulent reconfigurations of what it is that universities do.

A decade ago, Dearing (1997: 1) prefaced his report from the Committee of Inquiry into Higher Education with a quote from John Masefield, speaking at the University of Sheffield in 1946 on the purpose of a university:

> It is a place where those who hate ignorance may strive to know, where those who perceive truth may strive to make others see; where seekers and learners alike, banded together in the search for knowledge, will honour thought in all its finer ways, will welcome thinkers in distress or in exile, will uphold ever the dignity of thought and learning and will exact standards in these things.

Equally, at the same time, pressures of a different kind were making themselves felt with increasing urgency. For example, as Parker wrote, 'Under the pressure of publications hungry "line managers" in departments and faculties, students are rapidly becoming incidental to the work lecturers do and at times get constructed as impediments to it' (Parker 1997: 123).

Yet the purpose and process of teaching is never far from the lives of those who work in universities. As Hall puts it:

> We talk about intellectual practice as if it is the practice of intellectuals in the library reading the right canonical texts or consulting some other intellectuals at conferences. But the ongoing work of an intellectual practice for most of us (. . .) is indeed to teach (. . .) the first people we might make some connection with are our students. (Hall 1992: 290)

This sense of connection with students and the changes that this will wreak upon them has been a basic staple of thinking about the purposes of university education for some considerable time. For the Scottish scholar of the Enlightenment Hugh Blair for example, the purpose of university education was initially to have access to the wider, cosmopolitan world: 'in other words, a way to move past parochial standards towards universal principles of truth and beauty'. As well as this concern with universal issues, he also valued 'more local concerns over personal "reputation" and professional distinction' (Dosanjh 1998: 63, Valdes-Mirayes 2005).

A university may prepare students in the sense of giving them subject knowledge, but there may even be a strong desire to reconfigure the students' orientation to learning itself. We can see this in Dearing's (1997) notion that upon leaving higher education all students should have learned to take responsibility for their own learning. Each generation adds its own purposes and duties upon the shoulders of educators so that they are pulled in a variety of sometimes contradictory directions. In the twenty-first century, new duties have been found for the universities. McWilliam and Lee (2006) describe what they call 'fantasies about the role of education' in contemporary policy-making on education. The first of these is the hope on the part of governments and societies themselves that education should ameliorate social disadvantage, often in spite of the current political reality and the prevailing economic conditions. This 'redemptive fantasy permeates educational histories' (McWilliam and Lee 2006: 46) and leads into the second fantasy that education as a field, a discipline or an institution, can deliver these transformative learning outcomes all by itself. Education's incorporation of these fantasies corresponded to the rise in the twentieth century of a discipline of educational studies that was distinct from the process of merely training teachers. The enhanced role for education as an agent of social transformation was part of the discipline's striving to appear useful and links to the project of its disciplinarization within universities through the twentieth century (Green and Lee 1999).

The purpose of universities, and the nature of research on them and in them, will no doubt be increasingly conditioned by the commercial and corporate ethos that is developing in higher education in many nations. Boud and Tennant (2006: 294–5) itemize the pressures in this area in the following way:

1) There is a strong policy emphasis on the link between research, innovation and economic performance, so universities are now encouraged to become agents of economic regeneration. The

commercialization of research and the 'route to market' are now seen as important considerations in the justification of research funding, and there is a greater focus on identifiable research outcomes for both academics and doctoral students

2) There is a growing interest in the role of universities in producing workers for the new knowledge economy. The new knowledge economy involves the transformation of information rather than physical materials and requires high levels of education and responsiveness to change. Workers in such an economy are encouraged – and this is a role urged upon the universities too – to be creative, innovative, entrepreneurial, collaborative, flexible, self-motivated and self-managed, with a capacity for reflexivity (Usher 2002).
3) As a consequence, these qualities are increasingly finding their way into specifications of 'graduate attributes', and 'learning outcomes' at both undergraduate and postgraduate levels. Academics, too, are developing what has been termed a compartment as 'knowledge workers', with significant changes in the 'academic subject' identity being wrought (McWilliam 2003).
4) The production and distribution of knowledge is no longer the preserve of the universities (Nowotny *et al.* 2001). There is a growing recognition that performance-related knowledge is produced and situated in workplace context. Often this knowledge is not constrained by disciplinary boundaries; instead it is transdisciplinary (Gibbons *et al.* 1994).

This then unfolds a whole new topography of responsibilities, activities and outcomes in the higher education field, all of which have consequences for how we think about a university, what we think it does, and what we believe it is for. These changes also bring with them the possibility of new research questions, paradigms of enquiry and research programmes as we more formally and rigorously try to determine what is happening.

How we know about what is happening, and whether we get the chance to find out about it at all, depends to a substantial extent on what gets funded. Considerable amounts of time on the part of the university workforce are absorbed in the process of trying to get grants. Baez and Boyles (2002), through an analysis of the discourse of 'grants', suggest that 'academic capitalism' has become a way of life in universities. The deal has already been struck and our institutions have accepted the 'Faustian bargain' of the governmental and corporate embrace. What we imagine, think about and know about, is to a large extent made possible by the flows of funding.

However, even in the milieu of the corporate university it may still be possible to promote and undertake critical work. Indeed, with an awareness of the philosophical underpinning of enquiry it may even still be possible to find room for 'work which challenges the categories that organize [our] existence' (Baez and Boyles 2002: 45).

Learning to research in the social sciences has often been thought of as the mastery of technique. Tomes have been written and courses have been taught about issues such as sampling; questionnaire design; the management and analysis of data through computer packages like SPSS, SAS and Minitab; and the interpretation of confidence intervals, t values, F values and beta weights. Ominous role-plays have been staged where tongue-tied students interviewed one another in practice for the 'fieldwork' and workshops have been devoted to the correct preparation and annotation of transcripts.

Changing the researcher

Aside from the techniques and mechanics there is an increasing concern with the personal developments and 'soft skills' that are acquired by the researcher as they undergo this discipline of the self and learn to do research. Wood (2006: 54) summarizes some of the views about what research training is supposed to achieve. The 'learning outcomes' or the object of learning; for example could include:

1) The development of skills, for example social skills such as negotiation, listening, cooperating and empathizing. The

development of capacities and values across the whole research process, learned by 'contextualized doing' (Humphrey *et al.* 2001).
2) The reflexive integration of epistemology and technique (Jenkins 1995).
3) The acquisition of virtues and ways of thinking by 'looking hard' at them and using them (Wilson 1998).
4) Understanding the complexities of eliciting the views of others (Kushner 2000).
5) The acquisition of more than techniques, the extension of expertise and the development of the ability to evaluate one's own work and learning about oneself (Pearson and Brew 2002).

Thus, the researcher, like the reflexive self or the evidence-based practitioner, is exhorted to redesign herself or himself in the light of these new imperatives. Being a researcher, in this view, is about examining oneself, examining the ways in which one interacts with other people in the research process and in understanding the foundations upon which the techniques rest as well as the mechanical process of applying them. The research training is about a great deal more than simply learning techniques. That is why the philosophical attitude we have been encouraging in this book is so important. Left to itself, the development of theory in educational studies is somewhat haphazard. It has taken on a wide variety of meanings. It can include systems of evolving explanation, personal reflection, orienting principle, epistemological presupposition, developed argument and craft knowledge (Scheffler 1967, Chambers 1992, Thomas 1997, Thomas and James 2006). It is by appreciating the diversity of theoretical content, shapes and forms that the investigator can most fully understand the phenomena in which he or she is embedded in educational enquiry.

A further issue which we hope to have shed some light on is the relationship between claims about research 'quality' and the enthusiasm for randomized controlled trials in some quarters. This, as we have seen, is intimately linked to political agendas and to epistemological assumptions which have prompted a kind of cleansing process to rid the field of inquiries that do not look like experiments. Kaestle's (1993) article 'The Awful Reputation of Educational Research' has gained a reputation all of its own, and stands together with Hargreaves's speech as a means of naming and framing 'the problem' and posing 'solutions' (McWilliam and Lee 2006). The solutions include the intensely pragmatic and hyper-rational 'engineering' solutions proposed by Burkhardt and Schoenfeld (2003). The promotion of de-politicized ethical solutions in research continues (Hoestetler 2005).

The state of educational research and the links between research and policy reconsidered

The alleged shortcomings of educational research are deemed important because – allegedly – policy-makers want to make use of 'high-quality' research in order to deal with urgent problems. When we look more closely at the picture however, the relationship between research and policy is less clear. As McWilliam and Lee (2006) note, there is broad agreement that research could lead to some sort of improvement, in policy and practice, but it is far less clear what that improvement ought to look like. We are also handicapped because certain areas of enquiry, such as the management of educational change by managers and the policy-making process itself, is much less well understood. In Ball's (1990) monograph, *Politics and Policy Making in Education*, he claims that 'the basis for description of education policy has changed significantly and the established conceptual tools seem blunt and irrelevant' (Ball 1990: 8). Indeed, he later claimed that 'theoretical and epistemological dry rot [was] built into the analytical structures' (Ball 1994: 15) of policy research. Part of the problem was that policy studies in education were dominated by extremely pragmatic and project-oriented analyses from fields such as political science and public administration. These analyses were 'technocratic and managerialist in orientation and concerned mainly with implementation questions' (Lingard 1993: 36). This was the kind of approach that was lurid with complex and intricate arrays and coloured flowcharts of policy-making processes with a 'tend[ency] towards tidy generalities' (Ball 1990: 9) and seemed far removed from the human processes of getting things done. The audiences at conferences and seminars were treated to highly idealized, linear, two-dimensional representations of how policy was produced and implemented. Agreed values in one end, policy outcomes out the other (Gale 2005).

Ball struck out along a different trajectory, along the kinds of lines we have explored in this volume, to make sense of the policy process. Borrowing from cultural studies and Foucault, he set the agenda for a new generation of accounts of the policy-making process and its impact on education management and practice. Ball (1994) proposed that policy documents were both text and discourse and that they were 'cannibalized products' that carry meanings that represent the struggle and conflict that lay behind their production. Once this struggle is glossed over and the meanings are captured in policy documents themselves, they then become the focus of 'secondary adjustment' (Riseborough 1992), through a whole series of 'interpretations of interpretations' (Rizvi and Kemmis 1987) or 'refraction' (Prosser 1981, Freeland 1986). In this view, policy texts are themselves political acts or 'textual interventions into practice' (Ball 1994: 18), they '*enter* rather than simply change power relations' (1994: 20).

To emphasize the point, policy texts are both products and tools of production where 'the translation of the crude, abstract simplicities of policy texts into interactive and sustainable practices of some sort involves productive thought, invention and adaptation' (Ball 1994: 19). Moreover, they are not merely descriptive. As Gale (2005) notes, they are also 'practices that systematically form the objects of which they speak . . . [they] are not about objects; they do not identify objects, they constitute them and in the practice of doing so conceal their own invention' (Foucault 1972: 49).

Gorard (2006) notes that a peculiar thing about policy is that sometimes the time sequence is wrong for the standard policy causal model. Government policies do not necessarily pre-date the activities they are supposed to promote. The strongest trend towards wider participation in UK higher education occurred prior to the much-touted policies for widening participation. As

Gorard (2006: 19) suggests, 'perhaps policy is, on occasion at least, an epiphenomena providing a legislated basis for what already exists'.

This highlights another aspect of the reflective attitude which we have sought to promote in this volume. We wish to reassert the value of thinking about the aspects of the research context which are often under-studied and underdeveloped. By discussing the assumptions and philosophical and social bases of research we hope to have enabled the reader to pick out the areas which are glossed over or occluded in the official stories that are told about the process. We hope also to have emphasized that the philosophy of science is not an issue separate from research; it is an essential tool in understanding the debates and dilemmas surrounding educational research and it enables us to dissect out the issues behind contemporary concerns about 'research quality', evidence-based or evidence-informed practice and policy and the disagreements and discussions that are an essential part of the field.

In looking at the broad patterns of educational success and participation, it is clear that in the UK, as in many developed nations, a number of studies over the last half-century have shown that educational participation and outcomes are linked to time, place, social class, sex and family background (Gorard and Rees 2002).

To emphasize the importance of looking at the larger picture, and of appreciating the context, as we have identified at the start of this chapter, let us consider how this pattern of inequalities is also apparent, often involving the same people, in exactly the same way in other areas of public policy such as housing, health and crime. Those who appear to get the most out of the education system tend also to be those enjoying better health, living in more spacious housing and who are least likely to come into contact with the justice system as either offenders or victims. In the light of these persistent and pervasive inequalities, Gorard suggests that maybe education policy is generally so ineffective because the solution to these inequalities may not be educational at all (Gorard *et al.* 2004, Gorard 2006).

Thinking about research

However, we do not want to convey the impression that research is useless or that attempts to know the social world of education are futile. Gorard himself says that much can be done to improve education by promoting a culture which includes researchers and policy-makers in wanting to know what is happening and what the answers are, even where these are inconvenient for a theory, administration or ideology.

In this process, as Hammersley (2001) reminds us, a philosophically informed understanding can assist us in making a broad, well-informed judgement about the value and validity of the findings and conclusions of particular studies and in thinking through the question of how these relate to one another. These interrelationships between studies and forms of enquiry can be used to illuminate the research topic under investigation. This process – at least when it is at its best – involves the researcher trying also to make explicit their tacit knowledge, derived from experience, 'and to *think* about the substantive and methodological issues, not just to apply replicable procedures' (Hammersly 2001: 549). Our everyday understanding of the educational world is 'a kind of automatic integration of a very large number of data too fugitive and various . . . Our language is not meant to catch them' (Berlin 1996: 24). As Gadamer (1975: 251) puts it: 'the meaning exists at the beginning of any . . . research as well as at the end: as the choice of the theme to be investigated, the awakening of the desire to investigate, as the gaining of the new problematic'.

References

1 Theories of knowledge and theories of society

Appleby, J., Hunt, L. and Jacob, M. (1994) *Telling the Truth about History*. New York: W. W. Norton.

Baker, S. (2005) *Like a Fish in Water: Aspects of the contemporary UK higher education system as intended and as constructed*. PhD Thesis, University of Wales.

Ball, S. J. (2001) 'You've been NERFed! Dumbing down the academy. National Educational Research Forum "A national strategy – consultation paper": A brief and bilious response'. *Journal of Education Policy*, 16 (3), pp. 265–68.

Ball, S., Vincent, C., Kemp S. and Pietikainen, S. (2004) 'Middle class fractions, childcare and the "relational" and "normative" aspects of class practices'. *Sociological Review*, 52 (4), 478–502.

Barnett, R. (1997) *Higher Education: A critical business*. Buckingham: Open University Press.

Baty, P. and Shepherd, J. (2006) 'Ministers vilify researchers'. *The Times Higher Education Supplement*, 1 December.

Berger, P. and Luckman, T. (1966) *The Social Construction of Reality*. New York: Doubleday.

Bernstein, R. J. (1991) *The New Constellation. The Ethical-political Horizons of Modernity/Postmodernity*. Cambridge: Polity Press.

Blackmore, J. (2002) 'Is it only "What works" that "counts" in new knowledge economies? Evidence-based practice, educational research and teacher education in Australia'. *Social Policy and Society*, 1 (3), pp. 257–66.

Bloor, D. (1976) *Knowledge and Social Imagery*. London: Routledge and Kegan Paul.

Blumer, H. (1970) 'What is wrong with social theory?' in N. Denzin (ed.), *Sociological Methods: A sourcebook*. Chicago: Aldine.

Bourdieu, P. (1962) *The Algerians*. Boston: Beacon.

Bourdieu, P. (1977) *Outline of a Theory of Practice*. Cambridge: Cambridge University Press.

Bourdieu, P. (1986) 'Forms of capital' in J. Richardson (ed.), *Handbook of Theory of Research for the Sociology of Education*. London: Greenwood Press.

Bourdieu, P. (1988) *Homo Academicus*, P. Collier (trans.). Stanford: Stanford University Press.

Bourdieu, P. (1990) *The Logic of Practice.* Cambridge: Polity Press.

Bourdieu, P. (1996) *The State Nobility: Elite schools in the field of power,* L. C. Clough (trans.). Stanford: Stanford University Press.

Bourdieu, P. (1999/1993) *The Weight of the World: Social suffering in contemporary society,* P. Parkhurst, S. Ferguson, J. Emanuel, S. Johnson, S. and T. Waryn (trans.). Cambridge: Polity Press.

Bourdieu, P. (2000) *Pascalian Meditations,* R. Nice (trans.). Cambridge: Polity Press.

Bourdieu, P. and Wacquant, L. J. D. (eds) (1992) *An Invitation to Reflexive Sociology.* Chicago: University of Chicago Press.

Bowker, G. and Star, L. (1999) *Sorting Things Out.* Cambridge, MA: MIT Press.

Brookings Institution (1999) *Can We Make Education Policy on the Basis of Evidence? What Constitutes High Quality Education Research and How Can it be Incorporated into Policy-making?,* Brookings Press Forum, 8 December, http://www.brook.edu/comm/transcripts/19991208.htm.

Brooks, R. (2005) *Friendship and Educational Choice.* Basingstoke: Palgrave.

Brown, P. and Hesketh, A. (2004) *The Mismanagement of Talent: Employability and jobs in the knowledge economy.* Oxford: Oxford University Press.

Buchannan, D. R. (1998) 'Beyond positivism: Humanistic perspectives on theory and research in health education'. *Health Education Research: Theory and practice,* 13 (3), pp. 439–50.

Chouliaraki, L. and Fairclough, N. (1999) *Discourse in Late Modernity: Re-thinking critical discourse analysis.* Edinburgh: Edinburgh University Press.

Coles, R. (1989) *The Call of Stories: Teaching and the moral imagination.* New York: Houghton-Mifflin.

Craig, R. J., Clarke, F. L. and Amernic, J. H. (1999) 'Scholarship in university business schools – Cardinal Newman, creeping corporatism and farewell to the "disturber of the peace"?'. *Accounting, Auditing & Accountability Journal,* 12 (5), pp. 510–24.

Crowell, S. G. (1990) 'Dialogue and text: Re-marking the difference' in T. Maranhao (ed.), *The Interpretation of Dialogue.* Chicago: University of Chicago Press.

Davies, H. Nutley, S. and Smith, P. (2000a) 'Introducing evidence-based policy and practice in public services' in H. Davies, S. Nutley and P. Smith (eds), *What Works? Evidence-based Policy and Practice in Public Services.* Bristol: Policy Press, pp. 1–12.

Davies, H., Nutley, S. and Tilley, N. (2000b) 'Debates on the role of experimentation' in H. Davies, S. Nutley and P. Smith (eds), *What Works? Evidence-based Policy and Practice in Public Services.* Bristol: Policy Press, pp. 251–76.

Deem, R. (2006) 'Changing research perspectives on the management of higher education: Can research permeate the activities of manager-academics?'. *Higher Education Quarterly,* 60 (3), pp. 203–28.

Delanty, G. (2001) 'The university in the knowledge society'. *Organisation,* 8 (2), pp. 149–54.

Department for Education and Employment (DfEE) (2000) 'Blunkett Rejects Anti-Intellectualism and Welcomes Sound Ideas'. *DfEE News* 43/00. London: DfEE.

DiMaggio, P. and Powell, W. W. (1983) 'The iron cage revisited: Institutional isomorphism and collective rationality in organizational fields'. *American Sociological Review*, 48, pp. 147–60.

Drummond, G. (1998) 'New theorizing about organizations: The emergence of narrative and social theory for management'. *Current Topics in Management*, 3, pp. 93–122.

Espeland, W. N. and Stevens, M. (1998) 'Commensuration as a social process'. *Annual Review of Sociology*, 24, pp. 313–43.

Evans, J. and Benefield, P. (2001) 'Systematic reviews of educational research: Does the medical model fit?'. *British Educational Research Journal*, 27 (5), pp. 527–41.

Feuer, M., Towne, L. and Shavelson, R. (2002) 'Scientific culture and educational research'. *Educational Researcher*, 31, pp. 4–14.

Forsyth, A. and Furlong, A. (2000) *Socio-economic Disadvantage and Access to Higher Education*. Bristol: Policy Press.

Foster, S. (1986) 'Reading Pierre Bourdieu'. *Cultural Anthropology*, 1 (1), pp. 103–10.

Gadamer, H-G. (1979) *Truth and Method*. London: Sheed and Ward.

Geertz, C. (1973) *The Interpretation of Cultures*. New York: Basic Books.

Gitlin, T. (1991) 'The politics of communication and the communication of politics' in J. Curran and M. Gurevitch (eds), *Mass Media and Society*. London: Edward Arnold.

Grenfell, M. and James, D. (2004) 'Change in the field – changing the field: Bourdieu and the methodological practice of educational research'. *British Journal of Sociology of Education*, 25 (4), pp. 507–23.

Habermas, J. (1984) *The Theory of Communicative Action, Volume 1*. Cambridge: Polity Press.

Habermas, J. (1988) *On the Logic of the Social Sciences*. Cambridge, MA: MIT Press.

Hammersley, M. (2001) 'On "systematic" reviews of research literatures: A "narrative" response to Evans and Benefield'. *British Educational Research Journal*, 27 (5), pp. 543–54.

Hargreaves, D. (1996) 'Teaching as a research-based profession: Possibilities and prospects'. Teacher Training Agency Annual Lecture. London: Teacher Training Agency.

Hargreaves, D. (1997) 'In defence of research for evidence-based teaching: A rejoinder to Martyn Hammersley'. *British Educational Research Journal*, 23, pp. 405–19.

Heath, S. (2007) 'Widening the gap: Pre-university gap years and the "economy of experience".' *British Journal of Sociology of Education*, 28 (1), pp. 89–103.

Johnson, M. M. (1993) 'Functionalism and feminism: Is estrangement necessary?' in P. England (ed.), *Theory on Gender/Feminism on Theory*. New York: Aldine de Gruyter, pp. 115–30.

Keynes, J. M. (1936) *The General Theory of Employment Interest and Money*. London: Macmillan.

Kramnick, I. (1997) 'What do universities do?'. *Arts & Sciences Newsletter, Cornell University*, 18 (2), pp. 2–4, www.arts.cornell.edu/newsletr/spring97/spring97.htm.

Latour, B. (1987) *Science In Action: How to follow scientists and engineers through society*. Cambridge, MA: Harvard University Press.

Latour, B. and Woolgar, S. (1979) *Laboratory Life: The social construction of scientific facts*. Los Angeles: Sage.

Louden, W. (1991) *Understanding Teaching. Continuity and Change in Teachers' Knowledge*. London: Cassell.

Lyotard, J.-F. (1984) *The Postmodern Condition: A report on knowledge*. Manchester: Manchester University Press.

Meisenhelder, T. (1997) 'Pierre Bourdieu and the call for a reflexive sociology'. *Current Perspectives in Social Theory*, 17, pp. 159–83.

Nash, R. (1990) 'Bourdieu on education and social and cultural reproduction'. *British Journal of Sociology of Education*, 11 (4), pp. 431–47.

NERF (2000) *Research and Development for Education: A national consultation strategy*, www.nerf-uk.org/publicationsnetworks/subgroupreports/. (Accessed 20 December 2006).

Nespor, J. (2006) 'Morphologies of inquiry: The uses and spaces of paradigm proliferation'. *International Journal of Qualitative Studies in Education*, 19 (1), pp. 115–28.

Nutley, S. M. and Webb, J. (2000) 'Evidence and the policy process' in H. T. O. Davies, S. Nutley and M. P. C. Smith (eds), *What Works? Evidence-based Policy and Practice in Public Services*. Bristol: Policy Press, pp. 93–123.

Oliver, M. and Conole, G. (2003) 'Evidence-based practice and e-learning in Higher Education: Can we and should we?'. *Research Papers in Education*, 18 (4), pp. 385–97.

Parsons, T. (1937) *The Structure of Social Action*. Glencoe: The Free Press.

Parsons, T. (1951) *The Social System*. Glencoe: The Free Press.

Passmore, J. (1967) 'On teaching to be critical' in R. S. Peters (ed.), *The Concept of Education*. London: Routledge and Kegan Paul, pp. 192–212.

Potter, J. (1996) *Representing Reality*. London: Sage.

Power, S., Edwards, T., Whitty, G. and Wigfall, V. (2003) *Education and the Middle Classes*. Buckingham: Open University Press.

Reay, D., David, M. and Ball, S. (2001) 'Making a Difference? Institutional *habituses* and higher education choice'. *Sociological Research Online*, 5 (4), www.socresonline.org.uk/5/4/reay.html.

Reay, D., David, M. and Ball, S. (2005) *Degrees of Choice: Social class, race and gender in higher education*. Stoke-on-Trent: Trentham Books.

Rhoades, G. and Slaughter, S. (1998) 'Academic capitalism, managed professionals and supply-side higher education' in M. Randy (ed.), *Chalklines: The politics of work in the managed university*. Durham and London: Duke University Press.

Robbins, D. (1993) 'The practical importance of Bourdieu's analyses of higher education'. *Studies in Higher Education*, 18 (2), pp. 151–63.

Sackett, D., Rosenberg, W., Muir Grey, J., Haynes, R. and Richardson, W. (1996) 'Evidence-based medicine: What it is and what it isn't'. *British Medical Journal*, 312, pp. 71–2.

Scheuer, J. (2003) 'Habitus as the principle for social practice'. *Language in Society*, 32 (2), pp. 143–75.

Searle, J. (1995) *The Construction of Social Reality*. New York: The Free Press.

Shepherd, J. (2006) 'I felt very isolated, says stunned critic' in *The Times Higher Education Supplement*, 1 December.

Thomas, L. (2002) 'Student retention in higher education: The role of institutional habitus'. *Journal of Educational Policy*, 17 (4), pp. 423–42.

Traynor, M. (2000) 'Purity, conversion and the evidence-based movements'. *Health*, 4 (2), pp. 139–58.

Turner, F. M. (1996) *The Idea of a University, John Henry Newman*. New Haven, CT and London: Yale University Press.

United States Department of Education (2003) *Identifying and Implementing Educational Practices Supported by Rigorous Evidence: A user-friendly guide*.

Weaver, M. (2006) 'Do students value feedback? Student perceptions of tutors' written responses'. *Assessment and Evaluation in Higher Education*, 31 (3), pp. 379–94.

Weiss, C. H. (1979) 'The many meanings of research utilisation'. *Public Administration Review*, 39, pp. 426–31.

Whitty, G. (2006) 'Education(al) research and education policy-making: Is conflict inevitable?'. *British Educational Research Journal*, 32 (2), pp. 159–76.

2 The truth is out there? Positivism and realism

Ayer, A. J. (1959) *Logical Positivism*. London: Allen and Unwin.

Baert, P. (1996) 'Realist philosophy of the social sciences and economics: A critique'. *Cambridge Journal of Economics*, 20, pp. 513–22.

Ball, S., Macrae, S. and Maguire, M. (1999) 'Young lives, diverse choices and imagined futures in an education and training market'. *International Journal of Inclusive Education*, 3 (3), pp. 195–224.

Bates, I. and Riseborough, G. (1993) *Youth and Inequality*. Milton Keynes: Open University Press.

Bekhradnia, B., Whitnall, C. and Sastry, T. (2006) *The Academic Experience of Students in English Universities*. Oxford: Higher Education Policy Institute.

Benton, T. and Craib, I. (2001) *Philosophy of Social Science: The philosophical foundations of social thought*. Basingstoke: Palgrave.

Bhaskar, R. (1991) *Philosophy and the Idea of Freedom*. Oxford: Blackwell.

Bhaskar, R. (1997) *A Realist Theory of Science* (2nd edn). New York and London: Verso.

Bhaskar, R. (1998) *The Possibility of Naturalism: A philosophical critique of the contemporary human sciences* (3rd edn). New York and London: Routledge.

Binet, A. (1905) 'New methods for the diagnosis of the intellectual level of subnormals'. *L'Année Psychologique*, 12, pp. 191–244.

Blandon, J. Gregg, P. and Machin, S. (2005) *Intergenerational Mobility in Europe and North America.* London: London School of Economics, Centre for Economic Performance.

Brown, B., Crawford, P. and Hicks, C. (2003) *Evidence Based Research.* Maidenhead: Open University Press.

Brown, P. and Hesketh, A. (2004) *The Mismanagement of Talent: Employability and jobs in the knowledge economy.* Oxford: Oxford University Press.

Burns, R. B. (1997) *Introduction to Research Methods* (3rd edn). London: Longman.

Carnap, R., Hahn, H. and Neurath, O. (1973) *The Scientific World Conception: The Vienna circle* (originally published in 1929) in O. Neurath (ed.), *Empiricism and Sociology*, (trans. M. Neurath and R. S. Cohen). Dordrecht: Kluwer, p. 318.

Comte, A. (1976) *System of Positive Polity* (originally published in 1851) (trans. J. H. Bridges). New York: Burt Franklin.

Cross, R. T. and Price, R. F. (1992) *Teaching Science for Social Responsibility.* Sydney: St Louis Press.

Department for Education and Skills (DfES) (2003) *Foundation Degrees: Meeting the need for higher level skills.* London: DfES.

Department for Education and Skills (DfES) (2006) *Widening Participation in Higher Education.* London: DfES.

Duru-Bellat, M. (1996) 'Social inequalities in French secondary schools: From figures to theories'. *British Journal of Sociology of Education*, 17, pp. 341–50.

Elliott, J. (2006) 'Educational research as a form of democratic rationality'. *Journal of Philosophy of Education*, 40 (2), 169–85.

Elliott, J. and Doherty, P. (2001) 'Restructuring educational research for the "Third Way"?', in M. Fielding (ed.), *Taking Education Really Seriously, Four Years' Hard Labour.* London and New York: Routledge/Falmer, pp. 209–22.

Elster, J. (1989) *Nuts and Bolts for the Social Sciences.* Cambridge: Cambridge University Press.

Friedman, M. (1999) *Reconsidering Logical Positivism.* Cambridge: Cambridge University Press.

Gage, N. L. (1963), *Handbook of Research on Teaching.* Chicago: Rand McNally.

Garsten, C. and Jacobsson, K. (2003) 'Learning to be employable: An introduction' in C. Garsten and K. Jacobsson (eds), *Learning to be Employable: New agendas on work, responsibility and learning in a globalizing world.* London: Palgrave Macmillan, pp. 3–18.

Giroux, H. A. (1981) *Ideology, Culture and the Process of Schooling.* Philadelphia: Temple University Press.

Griffith, S. (2006) 'Pre-U – the new A-level?'. *The Sunday Times*, 26 November.

Hacking, I. (1981) *Scientific Revolutions*. New York: Oxford University Press.

Hankins, F. H. (1968), *Adolphe Quetelet as a Statistician* (originally published in 1908). New York: Arne Press.

Harding, S. (1991) *Whose Science, Whose knowledge? Thinking From Women's Lives*. Ithaca, NY: Cornell University Press.

Harvey, L. (1998) *Quality, Learning and Assessment*. Opening Keynote Address, 3rd Northumbria Assessment Conference: Quality and Standards in Assessing Student Learning, September, Newcastle.

Harvey, L. and Green, D. (1993) 'Assessing quality in higher education: A trans-binary research project'. *Assessment and Evaluation in Higher Education*, 18 (2), pp. 143–8.

Higher Education Funding Council for England (HEFCE) (2006) *Widening Participation: A review*. Report to the Minister of State for Higher Education and Lifelong Learning by the Higher Education Funding Council for England. London: Higher Education Funding Council for England.

Hillage, J. and Pollard, E. (1998) *Employability: Developing a framework for policy analysis*. Available online at: www.employment-studies.co.uk/summary/summary.php?id5emplblty. (London: DfES.

Houston, S. (2001) 'Transcending the fissure in risk theory: Critical realism and child welfare'. *Child and Family Social Work*, 6, pp. 219–28.

Houston, S. (2005) 'Philosophy, theory and method in social work: Challenging empiricism's claim on evidence-based practice'. *Journal of Social Work*, 5 (1), pp. 7–20.

Kamenka, E. (1983) *The Portable Karl Marx*. Harmondsworth: Penguin.

Kenwood, C. (1999) 'Social constructionism: Implications for psychotherapeutic practice' in D. Nightingale and J. Cromby (eds), *Social Constructionist Psychology: A critical analysis of theory and practice*. Buckingham: Open University Press, pp. 176–89.

Mackenzie, N. and Knipe, S. (2006) 'Research dilemmas: Paradigms, methods and methodology'. *Issues In Educational Research*, 16 (2), pp. 193–205.

Matthews, M. R. (2004) 'Reappraising positivism and education: The arguments of Philipp Frank and Herbert Feigl'. *Science & Education* , 13, pp. 7–39.

Mertens, D. M. (2005) *Research Methods in Education and Psychology: Integrating diversity with quantitative and qualitative approaches* (2nd edn). Thousand Oaks: Sage.

Mill, J. S. (1882) *Auguste Comte and Positivism*. London: George Routledge and Sons.

Milne, C. and Taylor, P. (1998) 'Between a myth and a hard place: Situating school science in a climate of critical cultural reform', in W. W. Cobern (ed.), *Sociocultural Perspectives on Science Education*. Dortrecht: Wolters Kluwer, pp. 25–48.

Moreau, M. P. and Leathwood, C. (2006) 'Graduates' employment and the discourse of employability: A critical analysis'. *Journal of Education and Work*, 19 (4), pp. 305–24.

Morley, C. (1897) *Studies in Board Schools*. London: Smith, Elder & Co.

Morley, L. (2001) 'Producing new workers: Quality, equality and employability in higher education'. *Quality in Higher Education*, 7 (2), pp. 131–8.

Munby, H. and Russell, T. (1998) 'Epistemology and context in research on learning to teach science' in B. J. Fraser and K. G. Tobin, (eds), *International Handbook of Science Education*, Dordrecht: Kluwer Academic Publishers, pp. 643–65.

Murphy, M. S. and Cooper, B. P. (2000) 'The death of the author at the birth of social science: The case of Harriet Martineau and Adolphe Quetelet'. *Studies in the History and Philosophy of Science*, 31 (1), pp. 1–36.

Nash, R. (2003) 'Social explanation and socialization: On Bourdieu and the structure, disposition, practice scheme'. *The Sociological Review*, 51 (1), pp. 43–62.

Nussbaum, M. (1990) *Love's Knowledge*. Oxford: Oxford University Press.

O'Leary, Z. (2004) *The Essential Guide to Doing Research*. London: Sage.

Philpott, H. B. (1904) *London at School: The story of the school board, 1879–1904*. London: T. Fisher Unwin.

Potts, P. (1983) 'Medicine, morals and mental deficiency: The contribution of doctors to the development of special education in England'. *Oxford Review of Education*, 9 (3), pp. 181–96.

Popper, K. R. (1959) *The Logic of Scientific Discovery*. New York: Basic Books.

Quine, W. V. O. (1990) *The Pursuit of Truth*. Cambridge, MA: Harvard University Press.

Read, J. and Walmsley, J. (2006) 'Historical perspectives on special education, 1890–1970'. *Disability & Society*, 21 (5), pp. 455–69.

Rorty, R. (1979) *Philosophy and the Mirror of Nature*. Oxford: Blackwell.

Rushton, J. P. (2002) 'New evidence on Sir Cyril Burt: His 1964 speech to the Association of Educational Psychologists'. *Intelligence*, 30, pp. 555–67.

Sarkar, S. (1996) *Logical Empiricism at its Peak: Schlick, Carnap and Neurath*. New York: Garland.

Schwandt, T. (2005) 'A diagnostic reading of scientifically based research for education'. *Educational Theory*, 55 (3), pp. 285–305.

Slavin, R. E. (2002) 'Evidence-based education policies: Transforming educational practice and research'. *Educational Researcher*, 31 (7), pp. 15–21.

Spearman, C. (1904) 'General intelligence, objectively defined and measured'. *American Journal of Psychology*, 15, pp. 201–93.

Terman, L. (1916) 'The uses of intelligence tests' in *The Measurement of Intelligence: An explanation of and a complete guide for the use of the Binet-Simon Intelligence Scale*. Boston: Houghton Mifflin.

Toulmin, S. E. (1969) *The Uses of Argument*. Cambridge: Cambridge University Press.

Travers, R. (ed.) (1973) *Second Handbook of Research on Teaching*. Chicago: Rand McNally.

Tysome, T. (2006) 'Access: must do better'. *The Times Higher Education Supplement*, 1 December.

Uebel, T. E. (1996) 'Anti-foundationalism and the Vienna Circle's revolution in philosophy'. *British Journal for the Philosophy of Science*, 47, pp. 415–40.

Yorke, M. (2004) 'Employability in higher education: What it is – what it is not'. *Learning and Employability Guides*. York: Higher Education Academy.

3 Interpretative approaches, ethnographies of higher education and the description of experience

Ashworth, P. D., Gerrish, K. and McManus, M. (2001) 'Whither nursing? Discourses underlying the attribution of master's level performance in nursing'. *Journal of Advanced Nursing*, 34 (5), pp. 621–8.

Baker, S. and Brown, B. (2007) *Rethinking Universities: The social functions of post compulsory education*. London and New York: Continuum International Publishers.

Baker, S., Brown, B. and Fazey, J. A. (2006) 'Individualisation in the widening participation debate'. *London Review of Education*, 4 (2), pp. 169–82.

Bamber, J. and Tett, L. (2001) 'Ensuring integrative learning experiences for non-traditional students in higher education'. *Widening Participation and Lifelong Learning*, 3 (1), pp. 8–16.

Barthes, R. (1982) 'Introduction to the structural analysis of narratives' in *A Barthes Reader*. New York: Hill & Wang, pp. 251–95.

Battiste, M. (2006) *The Global Challenge: Research ethics for protecting indigenous knowledge and heritage*. Keynote address, 2nd International Congress of Qualitative Inquiry, 4 May.

Berger, P. L., and Luckmann, T. (1963) *The Social Construction of Reality: A treatise in the sociology of knowledge*. Garden City, NY: Doubleday.

Bogdan, R. C. and Biklen, S. K. (1982) *Qualitative Research for Education: An introduction to theory and methods*. Boston: Allyn and Bacon Inc.

Bourdieu, P. (1986) *Distinction: A social critique of the judgement of taste*. London: Routledge.

Bowl, M. (2000) 'Listening to the voices of non-traditional students'. *Widening Participation and Lifelong Learning*, 2 (1), pp. 32–40.

Brown, P. (2005) *The Social Construction of Graduate Employability*. Final report to the ESRC. London: Economic and Social Research Council.

Brown, P., Hesketh, A. and Williams, S. (2004) *The Mismanagement of Talent: Employability and jobs in the knowledge economy*. Oxford: Oxford University Press.

Burman, E. and Parker, I. (1993) *Discourse Analytic Research: Repertoires and readings of texts in action*. London: Routledge.

Burr, V. (1995) *An Introduction to Social Constructionism*. London: Routledge.

Carey, J. W. (1989) *Culture as Communication*. Boston, MA: Unwin Hyman.

Carspecken, P. F. and Apple, M. (1992), 'Critical qualitative research: Theory, methodology and practice' in M. D. Lecompte, W. L. Milroy and J. Preissle (eds), *The Handbook of Qualitative Research in Education*. San Diego: Academic Press, pp. 447–505.

Clandinin, D. J. and Connelly, F. M. (2000) *Narrative Inquiry: Experience and story in qualitative research*. San Francisco: Jossey-Bass.

Collins, P. H. (2000) *Black Feminist Thought: Knowledge, consciousness and the politics of empowerment* (2nd edn). New York: Routledge.

Cotgrove, S. (1982) *Catastrophe or Cornucopia: The environment, politics, and the future*. New York: John Wiley & Sons.

Coulter, J. (1979) *The Social Construction of Mind*. London: Macmillan.

Cronbach, L. J. (1975) 'Beyond the two disciplines of scientific psychology'. *American Psychologist*, 30 (2), pp. 116–27.

Denzin, N. K. (1989) *Interpretive Interactionism*. London: Sage.

Denzin, N. K. and Lincoln, Y. S. (eds) (2000) *Handbook of Qualitative Research*. Thousand Oaks, CA: Sage.

Denzin, N. K. and Lincoln, Y. S. (eds) (2005), *The Sage Handbook of Qualitative Research*. Thousand Oaks, CA: Sage.

Denzin, N. K., Lincoln, Y. S. and Giardina, M. D. (2006) 'Disciplining qualitative research'. *International Journal of Qualitative Studies in Education*, 19 (6) pp. 769–82.

Dews, P. (1987) *Logics of Disintegration. Post-structuralist Thought and the Claims of Critical Theory*. London: Verso.

Dolby, N. and Dimitriadis, G. (eds) (2004) *Learning to Labour in New Times*. New York: Routledge-Falmer.

Dunphy, B. C. and Williamson, S. L. (2004) 'In pursuit of expertise: Toward an educational model for expertise development'. *Advances in Health Sciences Education*, 9, pp. 107–27.

Dyson S. and Brown, B. (2005) *Social Theory and Applied Health Research*. Maidenhead: Open University Press.

Edwards, R. and Mauthner, M. (2002) 'Ethics and feminist research: Theory and practice' in M. Mauthner, M. Birch, J. Jessop and T. Millar (eds), *Ethics in Qualitative Research*. London: Sage, pp. 14–31.

Eisner, E. W. (1991) *The Enlightened Eye: Qualitative inquiry and the enhancement of educational practice*. New York: Macmillan Publishing Company.

Eraut, M. (1994) *Developing Professional Knowledge and Competence*. London: Falmer Press.

Eraut, M. (2000) 'Non-formal learning, implicit learning and tacit knowledge in professional work' in F. Coffield (ed.), *The Necessity of Informal Learning*. Bristol: The Policy Press.

Evans, M. (2005) *Killing Thinking*. London and New York: Continuum International Publishers.

Frid, I., Õhlén, J. and Bergbom, I. (2000) 'On the use of narratives in nursing research'. *Journal of Advanced Nursing*, 32, pp. 695–703.

Furedi, F. (2004) *Where Have All the Intellectuals Gone?*. London and New York: Continuum International Publishers.

Garfinkel, H. (1967) *Studies in Ethnomethodology*. Cambridge: Polity Press.

Gergen, K. J. (1985), 'The social constructionist movement in modern psychology'. *American Psychologist*, 40 (3), pp. 266–75.

Gotham, K. F. and Staples, W. G. (1996) 'Narrative analysis and the new historical sociology'. *Sociological Quarterly*, 37, pp. 481–501.

Grande, S. (2004) *Red Pedagogy: Native American social and political thought*. Lanham, MD: Rowman and Littlefield.

Gray, R. E., Fergus, K. D. and Fitch, M. I. (2005) 'Two black men with prostate cancer: A narrative approach'. *British Journal of Health Psychology*, 10, pp. 71–84.

Hammersley, M. (1995) *The Politics of Social Research*. Thousand Oaks, CA: Sage.

Hammersley, M. and Gomm, R. (2000) 'Introduction' in R. Gomm, M. Hammersley and P. Foster (eds), *Case Study Method: Key issues, key texts*. London: Sage, pp. 1–16.

Hoepfl, M. C. (1997) 'Choosing qualitative research: A primer for technology education researchers'. *Journal of Technology Education*, 9 (1), pp. 47–63.

Howe, K. (1988) 'Against the quantitative–qualitative incompatibility thesis (or, dogmas die hard)'. *Educational Researcher*, 17 (8), pp. 10–16.

Hutchings, P. (ed.) (2000) *Approaches to the Scholarship of Teaching and Learning*. Menlo Park, CA: Carnegie Publications.

Hydén, L.-C. (1997), 'Illness and narrative'. *Sociology of Health and Illness*, 19, pp. 48–69.

Kilbourne, W. E. (1998) 'Green marketing: a theoretical perspective'. *Journal of Marketing Management*, 14 (6), pp. 641–55.

Kilbourne, W. E. (2006) 'The role of the dominant social paradigm in the quality of life/environmental interface'. *Applied Research in Quality of Life*, 1, pp. 39–61.

Knight, P. T. and Trowler, P. (2000) 'Department-level cultures and the improvement of learning and teaching'. *Studies in Higher Education*, 25 (1), pp. 69–83.

Kuhn, T. S. (1970) *The Structure of Scientific Revolutions* (2nd edn). Chicago: University of Chicago Press.

Langford, R. W. (2001) *Navigating the Maze of Nursing Research; An Interactive Learning Adventure*. St Louis, MO: Mosby Inc.

Lave, J. and Wenger, E. (1991) *Situated Learning: Legitimate Peripheral Participation*. Cambridge: Cambridge University Press.

Lincoln, Y. S. and Guba, E. G. (1985) *Naturalistic Inquiry*. Beverly Hills, CA: Sage.

Luck, L., Jackson, D. and Usher, K. (2006) 'Case study: A bridge across the paradigms'. *Nursing Inquiry*, 13 (2), pp. 103–09.

Lueddeke, G. R. (2003) 'Professionalising teaching practice in higher education: A study of disciplinary variation and "teaching-scholarship"'. *Studies in Higher Education*, 28 (2), pp. 213–28.

Maines, D. R. (1993) 'Narrative's moment and sociology's phenomena: Toward a narrative sociology'. *Sociological Quarterly*, 34, pp. 17–38.

Marshall, C. and Rossman, G. B. (2006) *Designing Qualitative Research.* Thousand Oaks, CA: Sage.

McDiarmid, G. (ed.) (1976) *From Quantitative to Qualitative Change in Ontario Education.* Toronto: Ontario Institute for Studies in Education.

Milbrath, L. (1984) *Environmentalists: Vanguards for a new society.* Albany, NY: University of New York.

Morley, L. (1999) *Organising Feminisms: The micropolitics of the academy.* London: Macmillan.

Murphy, P. (ed.) (1999) *Learners, Learning and Assessment.* London: Paul Chapman.

Paley, J. and Eva, G. (2005) 'Narrative vigilance: The analysis of stories in health care'. *Nursing Philosophy,* 6, pp. 83–97.

Patton, M. Q. (1990) *Qualitative Evaluation and Research Methods* (2nd edn). Newbury Park, CA: Sage.

Patvardhan, C. (2005) 'Tips on breaking bad news'. *British Medical Journal,* 330, pp. 1131.

Pickering, A. M. (2006) 'Learning about university teaching: Reflections on a research study investigating influences for change'. *Teaching in Higher Education,* 11 (3), pp. 319–35.

Potter, J. and Wetherall, M. (1995) 'Discourse analysis' in J. Smith, R. Harre and I. van Langenhove (eds), *Rethinking Methods in Psychology.* London: Sage, pp. 80–92.

Prince, G. (1991) *Dictionary of Narratology.* Aldershot: Scolar Press.

Ragin, C. C. (1992) 'Introduction: Cases of "what is a case"' in C. C. Ragin and H. S. Becker (eds), *What is a Case? Exploring the Foundations of Social Inquiry.* Cambridge: Cambridge University Press, pp. 1–17.

Reay, D. (2005) 'Beyond consciousness? The psychic landscape of social class'. *Sociology,* 39 (5), pp. 911–28.

Reay, D., David, M. E. and Ball, S. (2005) *Degrees of Choice: Social Class, Race and Gender in Higher Education.* Stoke on Trent: Trentham Books.

Richardson, B. (1997) *Unlikely Stories: Causality and the nature of modern narrative.* Newark, DE: University of Delaware Press.

Rimmon-Kenan, S. (2002) *Narrative Fiction* (2nd edn). London: Routledge.

Salomon, G. (ed.) (1993) *Distributed Cognition: Psychological and educational considerations.* Cambridge: Cambridge University Press.

Skelton, C. (2004) 'Gender, career and "individualisation" in the audit society'. *Research in Education,* 72, pp. 91–108.

Skelton, C. (2005a) 'The "individualized" (woman) in the academy: Ulrich Beck, gender and power'. *Gender and Education,* 17 (3), pp. 319–32.

Skelton, C. (2005b) 'The "self-interested" woman academic: A consideration of Beck's model of the "individualised individual".' *British Journal of Sociology of Education,* 26 (1), pp. 5–16.

Smith, J. (1983) 'Quantitative versus qualitative research: An attempt to clarify the issue'. *Educational Researcher,* 12, pp. 6–13.

Smith, J. and Heshusius, L. (1986) 'Closing down the conversation: The end of the quantitative–qualitative debate among educational inquirers'. *Educational Researcher*, 15 (1), pp. 4–12.

Smith, L. T. (2005) 'On tricky ground: Researching the native in the age of uncertainty' in N. K. Denzin and Y. S. Lincoln (eds), *Handbook of Qualitative Research* (3rd edn). Thousand Oaks, CA.: Sage.

Smith, L. T. (2006) 'Choosing the margins: The role of research in indigenous struggles for social justice' in M. D. Giardina and N. K. Denzin (eds), *Qualitative Inquiry and the Conservative Challenge: Confronting methodological fundamentalism.* Walnut Creek, CA: Left Coast Press, pp. 165–86.

Stake, R. E. (1978) 'The case study method in social inquiry'. *Educational Researcher*, 7 (2), pp. 5–8.

Stake, R. E. (1995) *The Art of Case Study Research.* Thousand Oaks, CA: Sage.

Stake, R. E. (2000) 'Case studies' in N. K. Denzin and Y. S. Lincoln (eds), *Handbook of Qualitative Research.* Thousand Oaks, CA: Sage, pp. 435–54.

Stallings, W. M. (1995) 'Confessions of a quantitative educational researcher trying to teach qualitative research'. *Educational Researcher*, 24 (3), pp. 31–2.

Strauss, A. and Corbin, J. (1990) *Basics of Qualitative Research: Grounded theory procedures and techniques.* Newbury Park, CA: Sage.

Thomas, L. (2002) 'Student retention in higher education: The role of institutional habitus'. *Journal of Education Policy*, 17 (4), pp. 423–42.

Trigwell, K. and Shale, S. (2004) 'Student learning and the scholarship of university teaching'. *Studies in Higher Education*, 29 (4), pp. 523–36.

Ussher, J. M. (1999), 'Women's madness: A material–discursive–intra-psychic approach' in D. Fee (ed.), *Psychology and the Postmodern: Mental illness as discourse and experience.* London: Sage, pp. 207–30.

Wenger, E. (1998) *Communities of Practice: Learning, meaning and identity.* Cambridge: Cambridge University Press.

Wittgenstein, L. (1958) *Philosophical Investigations* (2nd edn) (trans. G. E. M. Anscombe and R. Rhees). Oxford: Blackwell.

Wright, H. K. (2006) 'Are we (t)here yet? Qualitative research in education's profuse and contested present'. *International Journal of Qualitative Studies in Education*, 19 (6), pp. 793–802.

Yin, R. K. (2003) *Case Study Research; Designs and Method* (3rd edn). Thousand Oaks, CA: Sage.

4 Philosophies of research in education: Knowledge in education and knowledge of education

Beck, U. (1992) *Risk Society: Towards a new modernity.* London: Sage.

Berglund, A. (2004) 'A framework to study learning in a complex learning environment'. *Research in Learning Technology*, 12 (1), pp. 65–79.

Berry, G. (1996) *Improving Student Achievement through Behaviour Intervention.* EDRS: Microfiche [2 card(s)], Paper.

Biggs, J. B. (1987) *Student Approaches to Learning and Studying.* Melbourne: Australian Council for Educational Research.

Bleakley, A. (1999) 'From reflective practice to holistic reflexivity'. *Studies in Higher Education, 24,* 315–330.

Boud, D., & Walker, D. (1998) 'Promoting reflection in professional courses: The challenge of context'. *Studies in Higher Education, 23*(2), 191–206.

Bradbeer, J., Healey, M. and Kneale, P. (2004) 'Undergraduate geographers' understandings of geography, learning and teaching: A phenomenographic study'. *Journal of Geography in Higher Education,* 28 (1), pp. 17–34.

Britton, C. and Baxter, A. (1999) 'Becoming a mature student: Gendered narratives of the self'. *Gender and Education,* 11 (2), pp. 179–93.

Brookfield, S. (1995) *Becoming a critically reflective teacher.* San Francisco: Jossey-Bass.

Butler, J. (1990a) *Gender Trouble: Feminism and the Subversion of Identity.* London: Routledge.

Butler, J. (1990b) 'Performative acts and gender constitution: An essay in phenomenology and feminist theory' in S. E. Case (ed.), *Performing Feminisms: Feminist Critical Theory and Theatre.* Baltimore: Johns Hopkins University Press, pp. 270–82.

Cloonan, M. and Davies, I. (1998) 'Improving the possibility of better teaching by investigating the nature of student learning: With reference to procedural understanding in politics in higher education'. *Teaching in Higher Education,* 3 (2), pp. 173–83.

Cohen, L., and Manion, L. (1994) *Research Methods in Education* (4th edn). London: Routledge.

Coleman, J. S. (1991) 'What constitutes education opportunity?'. *Oxford Review of Education,* 17 (2), pp. 155–67.

Craik, F. I. M. and Lockhart, R. S. (1972) 'Levels of processing. A framework for memory research'. *Journal of Verbal Learning and Verbal Behaviour,* 11, pp. 671–84.

Crawford, K., Gordon, S., Nicholas, J. and Prosser, M. (1994) 'Conceptions of mathematics and how it is learned: The perspectives of students entering university'. *Learning and Instruction,* 4, pp. 331–45.

Crawford, K., Gordon, S., Nicholas, J. and Prosser, M. (1998) 'University students' conceptions of mathematics'. *Studies in Higher Education,* 23 (1), pp. 87–94.

Creswell, J. W. (2003) *Research Design: Qualitative, quantitative and mixed methods approaches* (2nd edn). Thousand Oaks, CA: Sage.

Dahlgren, L.-O. (1984) 'Outcomes of learning' in F. Marton, D. Hounsell and N. Entwistle (eds), *The Experience of Learning.* Edinburgh: Scottish Academic Press, pp. 19–35.

Dahlgren, L.-O. and Marton, F. (1978) 'Students' conceptions of subject matter: An aspect of learning and teaching in higher education'. *Studies in Higher Education*, 3, pp. 25–35.

Dewey, J. (1974) *Education: Selected writings*. Chicago: University of Chicago Press.

Ecclestone, K. (1996) 'The reflective practitioner: Mantra or a model for emancipation?'. *Studies in the Education of Adults*, 28 (2), pp. 146–61.

Edwards, R. (1993) *Mature Women Students: Separating or connecting family and education*. London: Taylor and Francis.

Eichelberger, T. (1989) *Disciplined Inquiry : Understanding and doing social research*. New York: Longman.

Entwistle, N. (1984) 'Contrasting perspectives on learning'. In F. Matron, D. Hounsell, & N. Entwistle (eds.), *The experience of learing* (pp. 1–18). Edinburgh: Scottish Academic Press.

Entwistle, N. J. and Entwistle, A. (1991) 'Contrasting forms of understanding for degree examinations: The student experience and its implications'. *Higher Education*, 22, pp. 205–27.

Eraut, M. (1994) *Developing Professional Knowledge and Competence*. London: Falmer Press.

Ericsson, K. A. and Simon, H. A. (1993) *Protocol Analysis: Verbal reports as data*. Cambridge, MA: MIT Press.

Foucault, M. (1972) *The Archaeology of Knowledge and the Discourse on Language*. New York: Tavistock.

Fransson, A. (1977) 'On qualitative differences in learning, IV: Effects of intrinsic motivation and extrinsic test anxiety on process and outcome'. *British Journal of Educational Psychology*, 47, pp. 244–57.

Gagne, R. M. (1970) *The Conditions of Learning* (2nd edn). New York: Holt, Rinehart and Winston.

Giddens, A. (1990) *The Consequences of Modernity*. Cambridge: Polity Press.

Gillat, A. and Sulzer-Azaroff, B. (1994) 'Promoting principals' managerial involvement in instructional improvement'. *Journal of Applied Behaviour Analysis*, 27, pp. 115–29.

Gray, J. (1992) *Men Are from Mars, Women Are from Venus*. London: Thorsons.

Gray, J. (1995) *Mars and Venus in the Bedroom: A guide to lasting romance and passion*. New York: HarperCollins.

Gunn, V. (2003) 'Transforming subject boundaries: The interface between higher education teaching and learning theories and subject-specific knowledge'. *Arts and Humanities in Higher Education*, 2 (3), pp. 265–80.

Hacking, I. (1995) 'The looping effect of human kinds' in D. Sperber, D. Premack and A. J. Premack (eds), *Causal Cognition: An interdisciplinary approach*. Oxford: Oxford University Press, pp. 351–83.

Hegarty-Hazel, E. and Prosser, M. (1991a) 'Relationship between students' conceptual knowledge and study strategies – Part 1: Student learning in physics'. *International Journal of Science Education*, 13 (3), pp. 303–12.

Hegarty-Hazel, E. and Prosser, M. (1991b) 'Relationship between students' conceptual knowledge and study strategies – Part 2: Student learning in biology'. *International Journal of Science Education*, 13 (4), pp. 421–29.

James, D. (1995) 'Mature studentship in higher education: Beyond a "species" approach'. *British Journal of Sociology of Education*, 16, pp. 451–66.

Kehily, M. J. (1995) 'Self-narration, autobiography and identity construction'. *Gender and Education*, 7, pp. 23–32.

Kroksmark, T. (1987) *Fenomenografisk Didaktik* (*Phenomenographic didactics*). PhD Thesis, Göteborg: Göteborg University.

Labowitz, S. (1967) 'Some observations on measurement and statistics'. *Social Forces*, 46, pp. 151–60.

Labowitz, S. (1970), 'The assignment of numbers to rank order categories'. *American Sociological Review*, 35, pp. 515–24.

Locke, E. A. (1996) 'Motivation through conscious goal setting'. *Applied & Preventative Psychology*, 5, pp. 117–24.

Locke, E. A. and Latham, G. P. (1990) 'Work motivation and satisfaction: Light at the end of the tunnel'. *Psychological Science*, 1, pp. 240–46.

Lonka, K. and Lindblom-Ylanne, S. (1996) 'Epistemologies, conceptions of learning and study practices in medicine and psychology'. *Higher Education*, 31, pp. 5–24.

Marton, F. (1981) 'Phenomenography – describing conceptions of the world around us'. *Instructional Science* 10: 177–200.

Marton, F. (1986) 'Phenomenography: A Research Approach to Investigating Different Understandings of Reality'. *Journal of Thought*, 2(3), 28–49.

Marton, F. and Booth, S. (1997) *Learning and Awareness*. Mahwah, NJ: Lawrence Erlbaum.

Marton, F. and Saljo, R. (1976). 'On qualitative differences in learning: 1 – Outcome and process', *British Journal of Educational Psychology* 46: 4–11.

Marton, F. and Saljo, R. (1976a) 'On qualitative differences in student learning, I: Outcome and process'. *British Journal of Educational Psychology*, 46, pp. 4–11.

Marton, F. and Saljo, R. (1976b) 'On the qualitative differences in learning, II: Outcome as a function of the learner's conception of the task'. *British Journal of Educational Psychology*, 46, pp. 115–27.

Marton, F. and Saljo, R. (1984) 'Approaches to learning' in F. Marton, D. Hounsell and N. Entwistle (eds), *The Experience of Learning*. Edinburgh: Scottish Academic Press, pp. 36–55.

Maynard, E. M. and Pearsall, S. J. (1994) 'What about male mature students? A comparison of the experiences of men and women students'. *Journal of Access Studies*, 9, pp. 229–40.

Mento, A. J., Steel, R. P. & Karren, R. J. (1987) 'A meta-analysis of the effects of goal setting on task performance: 1966–1984'. *Organisational Behaviour and Human Decision Processes*, 39, pp. 52–83.

Mertens, D. M. (2005) *Research Methods in Education and Psychology: Integrating Diversity with Quantitative and Qualitative Approaches* (2nd edn). Thousand Oaks, CA: Sage.

Modood, T. (2006) 'Ethnicity, muslims and higher education entry in Britain' *Teaching in Higher Education* 11(2): 247–250.

Nash, R. (1997) *Inequality/Difference: A sociology of education.* Palmerston North: ERDC Press.

Nash, R. (2003) 'Social explanation and socialization: On Bourdieu and the structure, disposition, practice scheme'. *Sociological Review,* 51, pp. 43–62.

Newton, D. P. and Newton, L. D. (1997) 'Teachers' conceptions of understanding historical and scientific events'. *British Journal of Educational Psychology,* 67, 513–27.

Newton, D. P. and Newton, L. D. (1998) 'Enculturation and understanding: Some differences between sixth formers' and graduates' conceptions of understanding in history and science'. *Teaching in Higher Education,* 3 (3), pp. 339–63.

Nisbett, R. E. and Wilson, T. D. (1977) 'Telling more than we know: Verbal reports on mental processes'. *Psychological Review,* 84, pp. 231–59.

Nuhfer, E. B. and Knipp, D. (2006) 'The use of a knowledge survey as an indicator of student Learning in an Introductory biology course'. *Life Sciences Education,* 5, pp. 313–16.

Pascall, G. and Cox, R. (1993a) 'Education and domesticity'. *Gender and Education,* 5, pp. 17–36.

Pascall, G. and Cox, R. (1993b) *Women Returning to Higher Education.* Buckingham: Society for Research into Higher Education and the Open University.

Pintich, P. and Degroot, E. (1990) 'Motivational and self-regulated learning components of classroom academic performance'. *Journal of Educational Psychology,* 82, pp. 33–40.

Preece, P. F. W. (2002) 'Equal-interval measurement: The foundation of quantitative educational research'. *Research Papers in Education,* 17 (4), pp. 363–72.

Prosser, M. and Trigwell, K. (1999) *Understanding Learning and Teaching: The experience in higher education.* Buckingham: Society for Research into Higher Education and Open University Press.

Provost, S. C. and Bond, N. W. (1997) 'Approaches to studying and academic performance in a traditional psychology course'. *Higher Education Research and Development,* 16, pp. 309–20.

Reay, D., Ball, S. and David, M. (2002) 'It's taking me a long time but I'll get there in the end: Mature students on access courses and higher education choice'. *British Educational Research Journal,* 28 (1), pp. 5–19.

Reay, D. (2003) 'A risky business? Mature working-class women students and access to higher education'. *Gender and Education,* 15 (3), pp. 301–17.

Renkl, A. (1997) 'Learning from worked-out examples: A study on individual differences'. *Cognitive Science,* 21, pp. 1–29.

Rose, N. (1990) *Governing the Soul: The shaping of the private self.* London: Routledge.
Sandberg, J. (1997) 'Are phenomenographic results reliable?' *Higher Education Research and Development,* 16(2), pp. 203–212.
Schön, D. A. (1983) 'Organizational learning' in G. Morgan (ed.), *Beyond Method. Strategies for Social Research.* Beverly Hills, CA: Sage, pp. 114–28.
Schön, D. A. (1987) *Educating the Reflective Practitioner.* San Francisco: Jossey-Bass.
Schutz, A. (1962) in M. Natanson (ed.), *The Problem of Social Reality: Collected Papers, Vol. 1.*The Hague: Martinus Nijhoff.
Shavit, Y. and Blossfield, H. P. (eds) (1993) *Persisting Inequality: Changing educational attainment in thirteen countries.* Boulder, CO: Westview Press.
Stevens, S. S. (1951), *Handbook of Experimental Psychology.* New York: Wiley.
Svensson, L. (1977) 'On the qualitative differences in learning, III: Study skill and learning'. *British Journal of Educational Psychology,* 47, pp. 233–43.
Taylor, G. (1993), 'A theory of practice: Hermeneutical understanding'. *Higher Education Research and Development,* 12 (1), pp. 59–72.
Tett, L. (2000) 'I'm working class and proud of it – Gendered experiences of non-traditional participants in higher education'. *Gender and Education,* 12 (2), pp. 183–94.
Trowler, P. and Cooper, A. (2002) 'Teaching and learning regimes: Implicit theories and recurrent practices in the enhancement of teaching and learning through educational development programmes'. *Higher Education Research and Development,* 21 (3), pp. 221–40.
Trowler, P., Fanghanel, J. and Wareham, T. (2005) 'Freeing the *chi* of change: The Higher Education Academy and enhancing teaching and learning in higher education'. *Studies in Higher Education,* 30 (4), pp. 427–44.
Webb, G. (1997) 'Deconstructing deep and surface: Towards a critique of phenomenography' *Higher Education* 33: 195–212.
Wellington, B. and Austin, P. (1996) 'Orientations to reflective practice'. *Educational Research,* 38 (3), pp. 307–16.
Wentzel, K. R. (1991) 'Relations between social competence and academic achievement in early adolescents'. *Child Development,* 62, pp. 1066–78.
White, F. (2002) 'A Cognitive-behavioural Measure of Student Goal Setting in a Tertiary Educational Context'. *Educational Psychology,* 22, (3), 285–304.
Wooton, S. (2002) 'Encouraging Learning or Measuring Failure?'. *Teaching in Higher Education,* 7 (3), pp. 353–7.

5 Evidence-based practice in higher education

Birnbaum, R. (2000) 'Policy scholars are from Venus; policy makers are from Mars'. *The Review of Higher Education,* 23 (2), pp. 119–32.
Bleakley, A. (2005) 'Stories as data, data as stories: Making sense of narrative inquiry in clinical education'. *Medical Education,* 39, pp. 534–40.
Boruch, R. and Mosteller, F. (2002) 'Overview and new directions' in F. Mosteller

and R. Boruch (eds), *Evidence Matters: Randomized trials in education research*. Washington: The Brookings Institution, pp. 1–14.

Burtless, G. (2002) 'Randomized field trials for policy evaluation: Why not in education?' in F. Mosteller and R. Boruch (eds), *Evidence Matters: Randomized trials in education research*. Washington: The Brookings Institution, pp. 179–97.

Clegg, S. (2005) 'Evidence-based practice in educational research: A critical realist critique of systematic review'. *British Journal of Sociology of Education*, 26 (3), pp. 415–28.

Clegg, S., Macdonald, R., Smith, K., Bradley, S. and Glover, C. (2004) 'Using research evidence to inform policy and practice within a university – the Sheffield Hallam University approach' in N. J. Jackson (ed.), *An Evidence-based Approach in Higher Education – How Far Can We Take It?* York: Higher Education Academy. www.heacademy.ac.uk.

Cochrane Collaboration (2007) www.cochrane.org/docs/descrip.htm.

Cochran-Smith, M. (2002) 'What a difference a definition makes: Highly qualified teachers, scientific researchers, and teacher education'. *Journal of Teacher Education*, 53 (3), pp. 187–9.

Coe, R. C. and Fitz-Gibbon, C. (2004) 'Evidence-based education: A view from the schools' system' in N. J. Jackson (ed.), *An Evidence-based Approach in Higher Education – How Far Can We Take It?* York: Higher Education Academy. www.heacademy.ac.uk.

Cook, T. D. and Payne, M. R. (2002) 'Objecting to the objections to using random assignment in educational research' in F. Mosteller and R. Boruch (eds), *Evidence Matters*. Washington: Brookings Institution, pp. 150–78.

Crawford, P., Brown, B., Anthony, P. and Hicks, C. (2002) 'Reluctant empiricists: Community mental health nurses and the art of evidence-based praxis'. *Health and Social Care in the Community*, 10 (4), pp. 287–98.

Cronbach, L. and Suppes, P. (1969) *Research for Tomorrow's Schools: Disciplined inquiry in education*. New York: Macmillan.

Danaher, G., Schirato, T. and Webb, J. (2000) *Understanding Foucault*. London: Sage.

Davidson, A. (1994) 'Ethics as ascetics: Foucault, the history of ethics and ancient thought' in G. Gutting (ed.), *The Cambridge Companion to Foucault*. Cambridge: Cambridge University Press, pp. 115–40.

Davydova, I. and Sharrock, W. (2003) 'The rise and fall of the fact/value distinction'. *Sociological Review*, 51 (3), pp. 357–75.

Derrida, J. (1976) *Of Grammatology*. Baltimore: Johns Hopkins University Press.

Dreyfus, H. L. and Dreyfus, S. E. (1986) 'Putting Computers in their place'. *Social Research*, 53, pp. 57–76.

Dreyfus, H. L. and Rabinow, P. (1982) *Michel Foucault: Beyond structualism and hermeneutics*. Chicago: The University of Chicago Press.

Dyson, S. and Brown, B. J. (2005) *Social Theory and Applied Research*. Buckingham: Open University Press.

Evans, J. and Benefield, P. (2001) 'Systematic reviews of educational research: Does the medical model fit?' *British Educational Research Journal*, 27, pp. 527–42.

Evidence for Policy and Practice Information and Co-ordinating Centre (2006) *EPPI-centre: Introduction*. http://eppi.ioe.ac.uk/EPPIWeb/home.aspx. (Accessed 27 December 2006).

Feyerabend, P. (1975) *Against Method: Outline of an anarchistic theory of knowledge*. New York: Columbia University Press.

Foucault, M. (1972) *The Archaeology of Knowledge*. London: Routledge.

Foucault, M. (1984) 'On the genealogy of ethics: An overview of work in progress' in P. Rabinow (ed.), *The Foucault Reader: An introduction to Foucault's thoughts*. London: Penguin, pp. 340–72.

Foucault, M. (1988) 'Technologies of the self' in L. H. Martin, H. Gutman and P. H. Hutton (eds), *Technologies of the Self: A seminar with Michel Foucault*. Amherst: The University of Massachusetts Press, pp. 16–49.

Foucault, M. (1998) 'On the archaeology of the sciences: Response to the epistemology circle' in J. Faubion (ed.), *Michel Foucault: Aesthetics, method, and epistemology*, vol. 2, New York: Free Press, pp. 297–333.

Fox, N. J. (2003) 'Practice-based evidence: Towards collaborative and transgressive research'. *Sociology*, 37 (1), pp. 81–102.

Garman, N. (1996) 'Qualitative inquiry: Meaning and menace for educational researchers' in P. Willis and B. Neville (eds), *Qualitative Research Practice in Adult Education*. Ringwood, VIC: David Lovell Publishing, pp. 11–29.

Geelan, D. (2001) 'Feyerabend revisited: Epistemological anarchy and disciplined electicism in educational research'. *Australian Educational Researcher*, 28 (1), 129–46.

Geelan, D. (2003) *The Death of Theory in Educational Research*, Proceedings of the 2003 Complexity Science and Educational Research Conference, 16–18 October, Edmonton, Canada, pp. 169–85.

Gherardi, S. and Turner, B. (2002) 'Real men don't collect soft data' in A. M. Huberman and M. B. Miles (eds), *The Qualitative Researcher's Companion*. London: Sage.

Gough, D. (2004) 'Synthesising and making accessible research evidence to inform policy and practice in higher education' in N. J. Jackson (ed.), *An Evidence-based Approach in Higher Education – How Far Can We Take It?* York: Higher Education Academy. www.heacademy.ac.uk.

Guba, E. G. (1981) 'Criteria for assessing the trustworthiness of naturalistic inquiries'. *Educational Communication and Technology Journal*, 29 (2), pp. 75–91.

Guba, E. G. and Lincoln, Y. S. (1981) *Effective Evaluation: Improving the usefulness of evaluation results through responsive and naturalistic approaches*. San Francisco: Jossey-Bass.

Guba, E. G. and Lincoln, Y. S. (1982) 'Epistemological and methodological bases of naturalistic inquiry'. *Educational Communication and Technology Journal*, 30 (4), pp. 233–52.

Guba, E. G. and Lincoln, Y. S. (1989) *Fourth Generation Evaluation.* Newbury Park, CA: Sage.

Hammersley, M. (2000) 'Evidence-based practice in education and the contribution of educational research' in L. Trinder and S. Reynolds (eds), *Evidence-based Practice: A critical appraisal.* London: Sage, pp. 163–83.

Holmberg, L., Baum, M. and Adami, H. O. (1999) 'On the scientific inference from clinical trials'. *Journal of Evaluation in Clinical Practice,* 5 (2), pp. 157–62.

Irigaray, L. (1985) *This Sex Which is Not One* (trans. C. Porter). Ithaca, NY: Cornell University Press.

Jackson, N. (2004) *Higher Education Academy Working Paper: The meanings of evidence-based practice in higher education: Themes, concepts and concerns emerging through public discussion.* www.heacademy.ac.uk/resources.asp?process=full_record§ion=generic&id=392.

Jackson, N. J., Gough, D., Dunne, E. and Shaw, M. (2004) *Developing the Infrastructure to Support an Evidence-informed Approach to Personal Development Planning.* York: Higher Education Academy.

Johnston, P. (2005) 'She boasted about binge drinking and "decking" officials in crude outburst. Now Blair promotes her to respect tsar'. *Daily Telegraph,* 3 September.

Knight, P. (2004), 'Reducing uncertainty' in N. J. Jackson (ed.), *An Evidence-based Approach in Higher Education – How Far Can We Take It?* York: Higher Education Academy. www.heacademy.ac.uk.

Lather, P. (2004a) 'Scientific research in education: a critical perspective'. *British Educational Research Journal,* 30 (6), pp. 759–72.

Lather, P. (2004b) 'This *IS* your father's paradigm: Government intrusion and the case of qualitative research in education'. *Qualitative Inquiry,* 10 (1), pp. 15–34.

Leask, M. and White, C. (2004) 'Using research evidence to improve teaching and learning' in N. J. Jackson (ed.), *An Evidence-based Approach in Higher Education – How Far Can We Take It?* York: Higher Education Academy. www.heacademy.ac.uk.

Levin, B. (2005) *Reforming Education: From origins to outcomes.* London: Routledge/Falmer.

Lincoln, Y. S. and Guba, E. G. (1985) *Naturalistic Inquiry.* Beverly Hills, CA: Sage.

Louch, A. R. (1967) *Explanation and Human Action.* Oxford: Basil Blackwell.

Lyotard, J. (1984) *The Postmodern Condition: A Report on Knowledge.* Minneapolis: University of Minnesota Press.

McBride, R. and Schostak, J. (1995) *An Introduction to Qualitative Research.* University of East Anglia Centre for Applied Research in Education. www.enquirylearning.net/ELU/Issues/Research/Res1Ch4.html.

Morris, C. (2004) 'Towards an evidence-based approach to quality enhancement – a modest proposal' in N. J. Jackson, *An Evidence-based Approach in Higher*

Education – How Far Can We Take It? York: Higher Education Academy. www.heacademy.ac.uk.

National Institute for Clinical Excellence (2007), www.nice.org.uk/Cat.asp?pn=public&cn=toplevel&ln=en.

National Research Council (2002) 'Scientific research in education' in R. J. Shavelson and L. Towne (eds), *Committee on Scientific Principles for Education Research.* Washington: National Academy Press.

Nicol, D. and Macfarleane-Dick, D. (2004) 'Building evidence to enhance students' learning: The SENLEF project' in N. J. Jackson (ed.) *An Evidence-based Approach in Higher Education – How Far Can We Take It?* York: Higher Education Academy. www.heacademy.ac.uk.

Oakley, A. (2000) *Experiments in Knowing: Gender and method in the social sciences.* Cambridge: Polity Press.

Olkowski, D. (2000) 'Body, knowledge and becoming-woman: Morpho-logic in Deleuze and Irigaray' in I. Buchanan and C. Colebrook (eds), *Deleuze and Feminist Theory.* Edinburgh: Edinburgh University Press, pp. 86–109.

Ollman, B. (2003) *Dance of the Dialectic: Steps in Marx's method.* Chicago: University of Illinois Press

Polanyi, M. (1983) *The Tacit Dimension.* Gloucester: Peter Smith.

Porter, T. M. (1995) *Trust in Numbers: The pursuit of objectivity in science and public life.* Princeton: Princeton University Press.

Ramsden, P. (2004) 'The Higher Education Academy'. *Exchange,* 6, p. 7.

Rose, N. (1990) *Governing the Soul: The shaping of the Private Self.* London: Routledge.

Schön, D. (1991) *The Reflective Turn: Case studies in and on educational practice.* New York: Teachers Press.

Searle, J. (1969) *Speech Acts: An essay in the philosophy of language.* Cambridge: Cambridge University Press.

Shaker, P. (2002) 'Is Washington Serious About Scientifically Based Research?'. Paper presented at Curriculum and Pedagogy Conference, Decatur, GA.

Shavelson, R., Phillips, D. C., Towne, L. and Feuer, M. (2003) 'On the science of education design studies'. *Educational Researcher,* 32 (1), pp. 25–8.

Stacey, R. D. (2000), *Strategic Management and Organisational Dynamics: The challenge of complexity.* London: Routledge.

Stern, D. T., Linzer, M., O'Sullivan, P. S. and Weld, L. (1995) 'Evaluating medical students' literature-appraisal skills'. *Academic Medicine,* 70, pp. 152–4.

Sweeney, K. G. and Kernick, D. (2002) 'Clinical evaluation: Constructing a new model for post-normal medicine'. *Journal of Evaluation in Clinical Practice,* 8 (2), pp. 131–8.

Tierney, R. J. (2001) 'An ethical chasm: Jurisdiction, jurisprudence, and the literacy profession'. *Journal of Adolescent and Adult Literacy,* 45 (4), pp. 260–76.

Torgerson, C. (2003) *Systematic Reviews.* London: Continuum.

Trinder, L. (2000) 'Introduction: The context of evidence-based practice' in L. Trinder and S. Reynolds (eds), *Evidence-based Practice: A critical appraisal.* London: Sage, pp. 1–15.

Usher, R. and Edwards, R. (1994) *Postmodernism and Education.* London: Routledge.

Van Maanen, J. (1988) *Tales of the Field: On writing ethnography.* Chicago: University of Chicago Press.

Whitty, G. (2006) 'Education(al) research and education policy making: Is conflict inevitable?'. *British Educational Research Journal,* 32 (2), pp. 159–76.

Widdershoven-Heerding, I. (1987) 'Medicine as a form of practical understanding'. *Theoretical Medicine,* 8, pp. 179–85.

Winch, P. (1958) *The Idea of Social Science.* London: Routledge.

6 Conclusion: Philosophies of research and philosophies of higher education

Baez, B. and Boyles, D. R. (2002) 'Are we selling out? Grants, entrepreneurship, and the future of the profession'. Paper presented at the Annual Meeting of the American Educational Studies Association, October.

Ball, S. (1990) *Politics and Policy Making in Education: Explorations in policy sociology.* London: Routledge.

Ball, S. (1994) *Education Reform: A critical and post-structural approach.* Buckingham: Open University Press.

Berlin, I. (1996) *The Sense of Reality.* London: Pimlico.

Boud, D. and Tennant, M. (2006) 'Putting doctoral education to work: Challenges to academic practice'. *Higher Education Research and Development,* 25 (3), pp. 293–306.

Burkhardt, H. and Schoenfeld, A. H. (2003) 'Improving educational research: Toward a more useful, more influential and better-funded enterprise'. *Educational Researcher,* 32 (9), pp. 3–14.

Chambers, J. H. (1992) *Empiricist Research on Teaching: A philosophical and practical critique of its scientific pretensions.* Dordrecht: Kluwer Academic Publishers.

Dearing, R. (1997) *National Committee of Inquiry into Higher Education.* London: DfEE.

Dosanjh, R. S. (1998) 'Blair's Lectures, Professionalism and Scottish Legal Education' in R. Crawford (ed.), *The Scottish Invention of English Literature.* Cambridge: Cambridge University Press, pp. 55–67.

Foucault, M. (1972) *The Archaeology of Knowledge.* London: Tavistock.

Freeland, J. (1986) 'Australia: The search for a new educational settlement' in R. Sharp (ed.) *Capitalist Crisis and Schooling: Comparative studies in the politics of education.* Melbourne: Macmillan, pp. 212–36.

Gadamer, H-G. (1975) *Truth and Method.* London: Sheed and Ward.

Gale, T. (2005) 'Towards a theory and practice of policy engagement: Higher education research policy in the making'. *The Australian Educational Researcher*, 33 (2), pp. 1–14.

Gibbons, M., Limoges, C. and Nowotny, H. (1994) *The New Production of Knowledge: The dynamics of science and research in contemporary societies.* London: Sage.

Gorard, S. (2006) 'Does policy matter in education?'. *International Journal of Research & Method in Education*, 29 (1), pp. 5–21.

Gorard, S. and Rees, G. (2002) *Creating a learning society?* Bristol: Policy Press.

Gorard, S., Lewis, J. and Smith, E. (2004) 'Disengagement in Wales: Educational, social and economic issues'. *Welsh Journal of Education*, 13 (1), pp. 118–47.

Green, B. and Lee, A. (1999) 'Educational research, disciplinarity and postgraduate pedagogy: On the subject of supervision' in A. Holbrook and S. Johnston (eds), *Postgraduate Education in Education.* Coldstream, VIC: Australian Association of Research in Education, pp. 88–104.

Hall, S. (1992) 'Cultural studies and it's theoretical legacies' in L. Grossberg, G. Nelson and P. Treichler (eds), *Cultural Studies.* New York and London: Routledge, pp. 277–94.

Hammersley, M. (2001) 'On "systematic" reviews of research literatures: A "narrative" response to Evans & Benefield'. *British Educational Research Journal*, 27 (5), pp. 543–54.

Hoestetler, K. (2005) 'What is "good" educational research?' *Educational Researcher*, 34 (6), pp. 16–21.

Humphrey, R. and Middleton, C., with Finnegan, R., Hemmings, S. and Phillips, D. (2001) *Learning to Research: Vol. 1, Reflection on Learning to Research.* Sheffield: University of Sheffield, Teaching and Learning Network for Sociology and Social Policy.

Jenkins, R. (1995) 'Social skills, research skills, sociological skills: Teaching reflexivity?' *Teaching Sociology*, 23, pp. 16–27.

Kaestle, C. (1993) 'The awful reputation of educational research'. *Educational Researcher*, 22 (1), pp. 23–31.

Kushner, S. (2000) 'The anthology of what's not worked before: The draft ESRC research training guidelines: Research intelligence'. *British Educational Research Association Newsletter*, 73, pp. 33–4.

Lingard, B. (1993) 'The changing state of policy production in education: Some Australian reflections on the state of policy sociology'. *International Studies in Sociology of Education*, 3 (1), 25–47.

McWilliam, E. (2003) 'Changing the academic subject'. *Studies in Higher Education*, 29 (2), pp. 151–63.

McWilliam, E. and Lee, A. (2006) 'The problem of "the problem with educational research"'. *The Australian Educational Researcher*, 33 (2), pp. 43–60.

Nowotny, H., Scott, P. and Gibbons, M. (2001) *Re-thinking Science: Knowledge and the Public in an Age of Uncertainty.* Cambridge: Polity Press.

Parker, D. (1997) 'Viewpoint: Why bother with Durkheim? Teaching sociology in the 1990s'. *The Sociological Review*, 45 (1), pp. 122–46.

Pearson, M. and Brew, A. (2002) 'Research training and supervisor development'. *Studies in Higher Education*, 27 (2), pp. 135–50.

Prosser, T. (1981) 'The politics of discretion: Aspects of discretionary power in the supplementary benefits scheme' in M. Adler and S. Asquith (eds), *Discretion and Welfare*. London: Heinemann, pp. 148–70.

Riseborough, G. (1992) 'Primary headship, state policy and the challenge of the 1990s'. *Journal of Education Policy*, 8 (2), pp. 123–42.

Rizvi, F. and Kemmis, S. (1987) *Dilemmas of Reform*. Geelong, VIC: Deakin University Press.

Scheffler, I. (1967) 'Philosophical models of teaching' in R. S. Peters (ed.), *The Concept of Education*. London: Routledge and Kegan Paul.

Thomas, G. (1997) 'What's the use of theory?'. *Harvard Educational Review*, 67, pp. 75–105.

Thomas, G. and James, D. (2006) 'Reinventing grounded theory: Some questions about theory, ground and discovery'. *British Educational Research Journal*, 32 (6), pp. 767–95.

Usher, R. (2002) 'A diversity of doctorates: Fitness for the knowledge economy?'. *Higher Education Research and Development*, 21 (2), pp. 143–53.

Valdes-Mirayes, J. R. (2005) 'The Prejudices of Education: Educational Aspects of the Scottish Enlightenment'. *Atlantis*, 27 (2), pp. 101–18.

Wilson, J. (1998) 'Preconditions for educational research'. *Educational Research*, 40 (2), pp. 161–8.

Wood, K. (2006) 'Changing as a person: The experience of learning to research in the social sciences'. *Higher Education Research & Development*, 25 (1), pp. 53–66.

Index